W9-CPE-799

THE COUNTRY HOUSE

THE COUNTRY HOUSE

Classic Style for an Elegant Home

Jenny Gibbs

Edited by Alison Wormleighton

WARD LOCK

EAST NORTHPORT PUBLIC LIBRARY
EAST NORTHPORT, NEW YORK

First published in the UK 1997
by Ward Lock
Wellington House
125 Strand
LONDON
WC2R OBB

A Cassell Imprint

Copyright © 1997 Jenny Gibbs

All rights reserved. No part of this publication may be
reproduced in any material form (including photocopying or
storing it in any medium by electronic means and whether or
not transiently or incidentally to some other use of this
publication) without the written permission of the copyright
owner, except in accordance with the provisions of the
Copyright, Designs and Patents Act 1988 or under the terms of
a licence issued by the Copyright Licensing Agency, 90
Tottenham Court Road, London W1P 9HE. Applications for the
copyright owner's written permission to reproduce any part of
this publication should be addressed to the publisher.

Distributed in the United States
by Sterling Publishing Co., Inc.
387 Park Avenue South, New York, NY 10016-8810
A British Library Cataloguing in Publication Data block for this
book may be obtained from the British Library

Designed by Isobel Gillan
Picture research by Emily Hedges

ISBN 0 7063 7575 0

Printed and bound by South China Printing Co. Ltd.,
Hong Kong

Contents

Introduction

Nothing is more evocative of the comfort and welcome of the country house bedroom than fresh white linen. Here the plump pillows and table cloth are trimmed with delicate white lace.

I t's not surprising that country house style is so well-loved, for it is a unique blend of two opposite and seemingly contradictory qualities: elegance and informality. Not only is this an intriguing mix but it is also certain to be a success, since it offers the best of both worlds with the drawbacks of neither. The combination of grandeur with down-to-earth practicality prevents it from being either stuffy or pedestrian. Add to that a patina of timelessness, warmth and individuality, and you have a truly irresistible style.

Of course, country house style is ideally suited to the large and dignified old stately home. But the beauty of this style is that it is so adaptable and individual. If your home has spacious rooms, high ceilings, large sash or mullion windows and interesting architectural features, it is tailormade for country house style. And if it doesn't, you can still use elements of the style to create a similar ambience – even if you live in a modern apartment in the middle of a city.

The architecture itself may well dictate the overall style, but where there is little architectural merit, the visual impact can be achieved by other means – whether it is a stunning window treatment or an array of interesting pictures. At the end of the day, real country house style involves a harmonious blend of architecture and decorative art.

Country house style is rooted deep in the past, having evolved over many centuries. It is also firmly based in the countryside: there is evidence everywhere of a love of the country and traditional country pursuits. Both of these factors help to account for its enormous appeal, because of their association with traditional values, stability, continuity and nature. The country house interior must be the most reassuring and inviting of all styles.

Perhaps just as important in its success is the fact that country house style is very easy on the eye. Mellow colours, polished wood, a glorious medley of textures and subtle patterns all blend together harmoniously. Yet there is enough character and quirkiness to prevent it ever looking predictable or bland.

The secret of successful country house style is to have two equally important priorities – quality and comfort. This is particularly important with furniture. As a general rule, the furniture in farmhouses has tended towards the rustic while manor houses have favoured more elegant furniture, often based on late eighteenth century styles. However, well-chosen contemporary furniture can also look stunning.

In fact, the occasional mix of styles skilfully done can look charming, and some contrast of finishes adds interest. Placing a deliberately distressed chest in proximity to an elegantly gilded piece, for example, can be very effective.

Part of the charm of the archetypal country house is that the furnishings look as though they have found their way there by accident. This is because furniture and ornaments from a variety of periods have been lovingly collected and handed down through the generations. Colours and patterns do not necessarily match or even co-ordinate, yet they form a subtle and harmonious whole. Combinations are sometimes distinctly odd – but they work.

Nevertheless, if you are setting out to create country house style, you won't have the luxury of letting it evolve naturally. Interior decorators go to extraordinary lengths to try to create this haphazard, artless look, so that even when the whole look has been put together with the utmost care, the atmosphere is that of a room that has evolved over time – a composite of ideas and past events.

This is why it's important for nothing to look brash or ultra-chic. There may even be small elements of shabbiness from constant use, and these generally enhance rather than detract from the romantic quality of country house decoration. It will appear elegant but well used and loved, and above all comfortable and welcoming.

This air of faded glory reinforces the enduring quality of country house style, while the juxtaposition of the realities of rural life with fine furnishings adds to the fascination. With its understated elegance, the country house is much more a family home than a showpiece, reflecting a relaxed but gracious way of life.

Country house style furnishings are traditional and elegant but simultaneously well used, comfortable and cosy.

The Development of the
COUNTRY HOUSE

A look at the development of the country house gives a fascinating insight into the widely varying influences that affected the style. It also provides a wealth of ideas, not only for inspiration, but also for ways of creating a convincing period look in keeping with a particular style of architecture. Similarly, some definitive styles such as Gothic are ideal for giving a featureless room a cohesive theme.

THE MIDDLE AGES

Country houses were initially the homes of those who ruled the land. The power of great landowners was formidable, and their homes were symbols of their power and wealth. During the Middle Ages – the Gothic era – the country house was the administrative centre of an estate, and the wealthy lived among their vast retinue of servants.

While medieval interiors were certainly not comfortable in the modern sense, they were highly colourful. In those unstable times, entire households moved around the country, from establishment to establishment. The servants would precede them and dress the house with splendid furnishings. Heraldic banners would be hung from the windows, and walls draped in tapestries or rich fabrics. Valuable tapestries were actually cut to fit the new room's dimensions and the window and door openings.

The largest houses were usually fortified and arranged around one or more courts, but they followed the same basic plan as smaller homes. Life revolved around the two-storey great hall, similar to the one in the photograph opposite. Here, lavish entertaining took place and meals were served to the entire household with ceremony. At one end of the great hall, there was a dais, or raised area, for the high table, where the owner, his wife and any important guests were seated.

At the other end of the hall, the front and back entrances faced each other. To prevent the inevitable draughts, a carved wooden screen was placed across the hall; the area behind it was known as the screens passage. A third door led from the screens passage to the service area, with the food preparation area, buttery, pantry and so on.

By about the fourteenth century, the house also included a number of other rooms. Beyond the dais end of the great hall were a parlour and, above that, a chamber which became known as the great chamber. In addition there were subsidiary rooms, such as a wardrobe, a privy and a 'closet', which was used for private devotions, study and business. These served as the family's private lodgings.

At the other end of the house, above the service area, was another chamber, again with subsidiary rooms, which served as

This fine example of a fifteenth century hall, at Penhow Castle, Wales, is typical of the medieval great hall, with its high open-beamed ceiling and large fireplace on one wall.

For centuries, the bed was the most important piece of furniture in the house, with rich and colourful hangings, as in this twelfth century example at Penhow Castle, Wales.

The long gallery at Haddon Hall, Derbyshire, is panelled in oak and walnut. The design of its beautiful Elizabethan plasterwork features quatrefoils, squares and leaf shapes.

guest lodgings. On the platform created by the screens passage was a minstrel gallery, where musicians would entertain the assembled family and guests. Ceilings were first introduced in the fifteenth century but generally during this period the roof timbers were exposed, as in the hall on page 9.

Windows, which were initially small, so as to be an effective defence against enemies and the weather, began to get larger from the mid fifteenth century. Glass, though prohibitively expensive, became more readily available at this time, and stained glass was sometimes used too. Lighting was by candles, which were considerably more expensive than the rushlights used by the less wealthy.

The floors in the larger country houses were often tiled, particularly red inlaid with

white. In the smaller country houses the floor might be of brick or beaten earth mixed with oxblood – which produced a hard, smooth surface that looked rather like quarry tiles – covered by loose rushes. The rushes were seldom changed, just added to. One contemporary account said that under the floor 'lies unmolested an ancient collection of . . . everything that is nasty' and others simply referred to it as 'the marsh'. (Carpets, introduced in the thirteenth century, were used on tables rather than the floor, not surprisingly.)

Simple wainscoting, or panelling, in the form of narrow vertical boards, colourfully painted, helped to insulate the walls. Walls that weren't panelled were whitewashed or covered with plaster of Paris and then decorated with freehand painting or stencilling. Often this included red lines simulating stonework, or colourful flowers or heraldic motifs.

Furniture was minimal. The dining table was a board on trestles, surrounded by benches and perhaps a few stools. The master of the house sat on a chair, and sometimes the most important visitor was honoured with a canopied chair. The bed was the most important piece, though even it was flimsy; the hangings were the most valuable part of it. The member of the household who 'upheld', or looked after, all these various draperies became known as an 'upholder', from which the term 'upholsterer' is derived.

THE SIXTEENTH CENTURY

The sixteenth century – the Tudor era, the last part of which was the Elizabethan period – brought a new peace and stability, which meant that households did not move around the country so much. Consequently, the furniture no longer had to be portable, and comfort and display became higher priorities.

Households were smaller and landowners generally sought a more private lifestyle, though they still entertained lavishly. By the mid fourteenth century the nobility were living in the private lodgings based around the parlour and great chamber. Within two centuries, the less wealthy had followed suit.

The layout of the sixteenth century house was not very different from that of the late Middle Ages. On the ground floor was the great hall, the importance of which gradually declined, until by the end of the century it was simply employed as a servants' dining hall and an entrance hall, apart from occasional use for special events or musical evenings.

At the dais end were one or more parlours. Serving as informal sitting and eating rooms, with an emphasis on intimacy as opposed to state, these became increasingly important through the century. The kitchen and related rooms still led off from the screens passage at the other end.

Upstairs, directly above the parlour, was the great chamber, now the most important ceremonial room of the house. By the middle of the century a withdrawing chamber usually adjoined the great chamber; gradually it began to be used as a private sitting, eating and reception room. Beyond that there might have been a bedchamber. Also on the first floor (or sometimes the second) there would be a gallery, which was a new development. This long, narrow room provided the perfect opportunity to display impressive paintings of one's ancestors.

Although the two-storey hall remained in some of the largest homes, its days were numbered. The growing use of chimney-stacks, which meant that the smoke from the fireplace no longer had to escape through the roof, allowed the 'ceiling over' of the great hall. The extra space upstairs could

then be devoted to enlarging the great chamber. With the new status of the great chamber, the staircase that led to it gained in importance too. Initially simple, narrow and made of stone, it was gradually replaced by a wide, beautifully carved oak staircase.

Floors were often of local stone such as York, granite, slate or marble. Brick was also common. As it is such a soft material it eventually disintegrated, so where brick is found in very old houses today it is probably a replacement. Glazed tiles were another option. Wide floorboards of oak and elm were mainly used for the upper storeys. Most floors downstairs were still covered with loose rushes or rush matting, a forerunner of the rush matting available today. Carpets were very rare and, if present at all, tended to be used as covers for tables or other furniture such as window seats, or as decorative hangings or curtains.

In large halls the roof timbers were still exposed, but most ceilings of the period were flat and the areas between the beams infilled with lath and plaster. Beams were not dark but a a mellow honey colour. The plasterwork itself became more elaborate during the century. A great variety of motifs were used, often executed in high relief and colourfully painted.

Walls were covered with oak wainscoting for up to three-quarters of their height. The wainscot was often beautifully carved and decorated with coloured designs. Early in the century, the characteristic Renaissance carving such as the linenfold pattern – representing linen arranged in vertical folds – and the interlaced designs known as strapwork had developed to a fine art. Later this was replaced by highly decorated or inlaid wainscoting.

Windows were now tall and elegant with leaded lights, though it was still only the wealthy who could afford glass. Interior shutters were used rather than curtains.

Tapestries were still used on the walls, but other hangings had also become very popular, including embroidered, appliquéd or leather hangings or rich textiles. Woollen, painted linen and stencilled hessian (burlap) hangings were found in bedrooms and in the smaller country houses. Surprisingly brilliant colours were used in all wall hangings. Biblical or mythological scenes, heraldic motifs, or floral or geometric patterns were often painted directly onto unpanelled limewashed plaster walls.

The freestanding furniture was designed to reflect the status of the owner. Very heavy, it was made of oak, ash or elm, and would be carved, inlaid or painted. The benches, stools and limited number of chairs for seating were still very uncomfortable, but cushions were increasingly used to remedy this. Dining tables were massive and there were a number of storage cupboards and chests.

Built-in furniture was a significant feature of sixteenth century houses. Cupboards were simply created by placing a frame and doors in front of a wall recess. Fixed benches were often placed in window recesses or within fireplace inglenooks. These first settles would sometimes have hinged tops so they could double as storage chests.

Country house lighting at this time generally consisted of candles supported in an iron holder, which would be placed on a table or chest. In grander homes, white candles were fixed in silver or pewter candlesticks or sometimes in candlestands of brass or iron, then suspended from the ceiling on a pulley rope or chains – an early form of chandelier.

The carved and embellished oak panelling in the great parlour at Speke Hall, Merseyside, a Tudor manor house, dates from the mid sixteenth century. The heavy plasterwork ceiling is Jacobean. In the sixteenth century, carpet would have been used on the table but not on the floor.

THE SEVENTEENTH CENTURY

The seventeenth century was the Stuart era in Britain. The style of country houses at the beginning of the century, during the Jacobean period, was a more elaborate version of Tudor style. By the middle of the century, however, major changes were taking place and architecture began to take on a more classical form.

The chief exponent of this was the architect Inigo Jones, who was influenced by the sixteenth century Venetian architect Palladio. Jones is regarded as having been the founder of English classical architecture. However, the Palladian style he introduced did not become widespread until the early eighteenth century (see page 18).

The Baroque style, which started in Italy, spread through Europe during the seventeenth century. Around 1660, at the beginning of the Restoration period, it reached Britain by way of Holland and France, where, as the Louis XIV style, it had become more classical. By the William and Mary period at the end of the century, English Baroque was fully developed.

The architects most associated with the English Baroque were Sir Christopher Wren, Sir Roger Pratt and Sir John Vanbrugh, who were heavily influenced by Louis XIV's Versailles. Wren's rebuilt Hampton Court, Pratt's Coleshill and Vanbrugh's Castle Howard and Blenheim Palace were prototypes for other, smaller Baroque country houses.

The Baroque style became the basis for modern ideas of interior decoration. The walls were divided into sections – cornice (crown molding), frieze, picture rail, infill

The intricately carved panels on the doors and the staircase at Ham House, a seventeenth century country house in Surrey, were grained and gilded in a way that was probably derived from decorative strapwork.

(or field), chair rail, dado (wainscot) and skirting (baseboard) – corresponding to the sections of the classical column.

Baroque houses were laid out in much the same pattern all over Europe, and small country houses followed the new formal plan, too, albeit in a smaller way. The need to make the facades of the houses as symmetrical as possible dictated the interior layout to some extent.

The great chamber, now called the saloon, and the main parlour were moved from their positions at one end of the hall – on the first floor and ground floor respectively – to the centre. The parlour was entered from the hall, and a splendid staircase led to the saloon. However, from the end of the century the saloon was increasingly found on the ground floor, having supplanted the main parlour.

Off the saloon was a withdrawing room. On one side of the saloon were the family's lodgings, which were now known as apartments and which included an informal parlour, called the common parlour. On the other side were the guests' apartments.

Servants were moved out of the great hall into one of their own. The great hall, which had a grand staircase – now in beautifully carved and painted wood, rather than stone – leading to the first floor, had become effectively nothing more than a vestibule, albeit a grand one. (That said, many country houses did, in fact, retain their large, two-storey halls well into the next century, still using them for the occasional large function and retaining their traditional decor.)

Services were now in the basement, though from the end of the century the kitchen was sometimes housed in a separate pavilion. Servants' quarters were in the basement or side wings, and backstairs were built to try to keep the everyday workings of the house out of sight.

The kitchen at Ham House shows the way in which cooking was carried out in the seventeenth century. It was done at an open fireplace with a clockwork spit to roast the meat and special braziers for boiling cauldrons. The servants would have eaten at the kitchen table which is shown here laid with pewter ware.

The guiding principle of the Baroque house was that the greater the degree of intimacy of visitors with the occupants, the deeper into the house they were allowed. In a grand country house, as one progressed through the series of rooms along the so-called 'axis of honour', they became smaller and more richly furnished. The room beyond the bedchamber – the closet, which was by then sometimes called the cabinet – became the inner sanctum, with the finest paintings, porcelain and textiles. (The king used his cabinet for meetings of his inner council, which was the precursor of today's government cabinet.)

Ornate plasterwork standing out in strong relief was a feature of Baroque-influenced interiors, as can be seen from this hand-some fireplace at Blickling Hall in Norfolk.

The line of interconnecting state rooms was known as an *enfilade*, which meant a 'file of rooms'. All the doors aligned, creating an impressive vista and processional route. The visitor would start at the great chamber (also known as the state dining room), proceed to the anteroom (now called the state drawing room), go on to the withdrawing or presence chamber (also called the state music room), eventually reach the bedchamber with its balustraded bed, and finish – if very honoured – in the closet.

Most grand country houses were sumptuously decorated, to the point of being theatrical and grandiose. Walls had rectilinear panelling with raised mouldings, sometimes carved and enriched with gilding. Often woodwork was painted to imitate marble, expensive woods or exotic materials such as lapis lazuli. Intricate limewood carving on chimneypieces, pediments, staircases and panelling depicted festoons of fruit and foliage. The ceilings were decorated with allegorical paintings of

This magnificent bedroom at Ham House is decorated en suite, *in the style of the late seventeenth and early eighteenth centuries, with chair covers, and in this instance the wall-coverings as well, designed to match the magnificent bed-hangings. The domed bed canopy and use of edging and tassels were very typical of the period.*

classical subjects, or ornate plasterwork, and the cornice had recently been introduced.

All this formed a splendid background to silvered or inlaid furniture, Oriental lacquerware, Delft and Chinese porcelain and an abundance of fine textiles and wall hangings. Huge pier-glasses (mirrors) hung between shuttered sash windows (introduced this century). Floorboards were still common, and polished parquet flooring was introduced. Tiles and stone were also used, and sometimes marble. Oriental rugs were for the first time used on the floors. Lighting was still by candles, which were held in wall sconces and in painted or gilded wood (or occasionally crystal or silver) chandeliers.

Less grand country houses still had whitewashed plaster walls, often with textile hangings or blockprinted wallpaper. The ceilings were decorated with round or oblong plasterwork depicting swags of fruit and flowers. Floors in the less formal rooms of these houses were still covered with rush matting, though loose rushes had been abandoned. Turkeywork (hand-knotted wool imitating rugs from Turkey or Persia) provided a colourful upholstery fabric.

Furniture was beginning to get lighter, and walnut replaced oak. Comfort was increasingly a priority, with well-padded chairs appearing during the last quarter of the century. The furniture was still arranged formally against the wall. The dining table was now either a refectory or a draw-leaf style, but diners still sat on small stools or low benches. Other typical furniture included high-backed chairs, chests of drawers, cabinets-on-stands, bookcases, tea-tables and card-tables. Beds were taller and more splendid than ever, as can be seen in the example on the left.

Bed hangings were magnificent now too. By the second half of the century even windows had single rudimentary curtains. By the end of the century, pairs of curtains were in use, and some of the wealthiest homes were using silk pull-up curtains, the forerunners of today's Austrian blinds (shades). Most windows were glazed by this time.

THE EARLY EIGHTEENTH CENTURY

Early in the eighteenth century, during the brief reign of Queen Anne and then during the Early Georgian period, the Baroque went out of fashion. It was replaced by a trend towards elegance and restraint, and a new classical style known as the Palladian revival (or simply the Palladian style). This style was based on the ideas of the seventeenth century architect Inigo Jones and the sixteenth century Venetian architect Andrea Palladio. The architect William Kent and his patron Lord Burlington were the main influences in this.

Kent was the first architect to take responsibility for all the interior details as well as the architecture, setting a new trend. He designed some memorable furniture to suit Palladio's architecture. For the first time there was a set of guidelines relating to interiors. Rooms were seen in mathematical terms, as cubes, one-and-a-half cubes or double cubes, with specified proportions.

The formal plan of the Palladian house was much the same as for the Baroque house. The hall, and the saloon leading off of it, were at the centre of the main floor; this was known as the *piano nobile*, which meant 'noble floor'. They were flanked by a state apartment and a private apartment each of which incorporated a withdrawing chamber, a bedchamber and a closet. On the outside, a portico (a classical style of porch, with columns and pediment resembling a Greek temple) fronted the entrance hall. An external flight of steps led up to the entrance.

Beneath the *piano nobile* was the 'rustic', the name for the lower storey, which could be described as a basement that was above ground, or a very squat ground floor. It contained the service area and, usually, some informal living rooms. All Palladian country houses, large or small, followed versions of this basic plan.

An innovation at the beginning of the century was the corridor, which ran parallel to the line of interconnecting state rooms. A kind of grand passage, it provided a handsome alternative route for parading through the rooms, as well as more convenient access to individual rooms. Corridors continued to be added to existing country houses over the next century.

The Palladian country house was formal and dignified, although furniture, mouldings and cornices (crown moldings) were lighter than their Baroque predecessors. Walnut was initially the principal wood, but mahogany was introduced in about 1725 and eventually replaced walnut. Gradually the amount of wood was reduced in favour of plasterwork.

Wood panelling to the full height of the room, with wooden mouldings added, was popular until around 1740. It was occasionally mahogany but more often a softwood that was painted in muted colours such as stone, drab or olive, with off-white mouldings sometimes picked out with gilt. Chocolate brown was a practical choice for internal woodwork such as doors and skirtings. In the 1730s, flat-painted white panelling with gilded mouldings became fashionable for grand drawing rooms and ballrooms.

Walls that were not panelled or papered were painted in vivid colours like crimson, acid green, brilliant blue or pink, using an eggshell-like paint with a sheen. Decorative paint finishes such as graining or marbling were other ways of decorating the panelling. Sometimes walls were just panelled up to chair rail height and the area above was covered with tapestry, silk brocade or damask, with a decorative fillet around the edges.

Mouldings with classical motifs were extensively used. Doors, overmantels bookcases, desks and other cased items were often 'architectural', with classical columns or pilasters and broken pediments. The tall sash windows were still just shuttered or covered with a simple pull-up curtain.

Ceilings were treated similarly, with the mouldings in gold and a white or coloured background. A characteristic ceiling of the period would be divided with a pattern of battens covered with plaster and decorated with mouldings around the edge, often with a circular element in the centre. It was typically whitewashed and picked out in sky blue. Reliefwork became much more shallow, and, as the century progressed, was replaced by flowing Rococo designs of natural forms.

Country house floors became more and more elaborate, with black-and-white paved squares, inlaid marble work and complicated

The plasterwork on the ceiling and cornice of a splendid reception room, c. 1737, at Newbridge House, Ireland, illustrates the more flowing designs that were carried out as a result of the influence of the Rococo style.

trompe l'oeil patterns. In some less important rooms, oak or pine floorboards were often left untreated and scrubbed or scoured with sand. Oriental carpets and rugs remained very much in fashion.

Furniture, though increasingly comfortable, was still arranged around the edge of the room. Chairs, no longer high-backed, had upholstered backs as well as seats. Massive carved gilt furniture was used for state rooms.

As before, lighting was by candles. Chandeliers were still most often made of painted or gilt wood and only held a few candles. Candles were also placed in girandoles, or branches, attached to wall brackets or mirrors.

THE MID EIGHTEENTH CENTURY

Towards the end of the Palladian revival, in the Mid Georgian period, the layout of the country house underwent some major changes. People were now spending more time in the public rooms and less in their private apartments. Balls and assemblies were being held in some of the larger houses. Consequently, some of the rooms that made up the state and family apartments had been absorbed into the public rooms of the house.

The drawing room, for example, which had once been a withdrawing room attached to an individual bedroom, was now an important room in its own right. The saloon was still used for dancing, but no longer for meals – there was now a separate dining room, roughly the same size as the drawing room. Larger houses also had an informal parlour for family meals.

Private apartments were now smaller, and there were more of them. Most just consisted of a bedroom and a dressing room, and possibly also a closet. Dressing rooms were, however, like private sitting rooms, often larger than the bedroom itself.

Although the Rococo style did not really catch on in England, the offshoot of it known as the 'Chinese taste', and later as Chinoiserie, was highly fashionable in the mid eighteenth century, particularly for bedrooms. This is the Chinese Bedroom at Badminton House, Gloucestershire.

Whereas previously the enfiladed rooms had been in a straight line, they were now arranged in a circle around an elegant circular staircase, which was lit from the top and cantilevered. People went up the staircase, through several reception rooms in a circular route and back down the stairs again.

Country houses still had a rustic (see page 18), where the servants' hall, butler's and housekeeper's rooms and cellars were located. There were still usually family rooms in the rustic, which might include the informal parlour, a smoking parlour, a billiard room, a study or even the owner's private apartment. The servants' sleeping quarters might be here or they might be at the top of the house or over the stable. The kitchen too might be in the rustic, or it might be in a completely separate pavilion.

The Palladian style was found only in Britain and America (see page 38). In continental Europe, Baroque developed into the Rococo style, also known as Louis XV for the French monarch under whom it flourished. This lighthearted, frivolous style never really caught on in England, but two of its offshoots – 'the Chinese taste', or

Chinoiserie, and 'the Gothic taste', sometimes spelled 'Gothick' – showed up in furniture and decoration. These romanticized, inaccurate versions of distant Cathay and the equally distant Middle Ages added a much-needed light touch to the otherwise very sober Palladian style. The highly influential furniture designer Thomas Chippendale worked in Rococo, Gothick and Chinese ('Chinese Chippendale') styles.

After panelling became less fashionable around 1740, the walls tended to be covered in damask or velvet, with matching curtains and upholstery. Alternatively, they might be papered – flocked wallpaper was fashionable for the best rooms, and hand-painted Chinese paper (or imitations) for the bedrooms. Stucco, a method of plaster decoration used for walls and ceilings, was a popular choice for the main living rooms.

Apart from the Gothic and Chinese styles of decor, mid eighteenth century rooms remained much the same as those from the earlier part of the century. Light colours such as pea green, sky blue, yellow and deep green were fashionable, but by now the finish was completely matt.

Hand-painted panels like these in Bernshammar, Sweden, imitating paintings from Pompeii were found in wealthy homes of the late eighteenth century all around Europe. They depicted classical arabesques, which are fanciful vertical patterns incorporating animals, figures, vases, fruit and foliage. Many wallpapers used very similar ornament and colours.

THE LATE EIGHTEENTH CENTURY

By the late eighteenth century, the Late Georgian period, the upper classes had developed a new enthusiasm for country life and its pursuits, and the house party had become the fashionable way to entertain. Not only had the functions and layouts of the rooms in the country house changed, so had the architectural style.

In Britain and Europe the prevailing style of the second half of the eighteenth century was neoclassical – in architectural terms, Greek revival. Thirty years later the style also reached America (see page 41). In Britain it was a reaction against the restraints of Palladian style, and on the continent a reaction against Rococo.

Neoclassicism was cool and elegant, with simple geometric forms and classical ornament. It sought inspiration directly from Greek and Roman architecture, bypassing the interpretations of intermediaries like Palladio.

The architect Robert Adam was at the forefront of these changes, which resulted in lighter, less decorated buildings. Adam brought a new charm and grace to his adaptations of classical styles. He used colour in a very distinctive way. The ceiling was the dominant feature of many of his rooms, and he applied a richly coloured background to it, picking out the delicate, low-relief plasterwork details in white or a strong colour.

His palette included pale and medium green, lilac, apricot and opal tints, and a stronger range of blues, greens, pinks and terracotta. (The terracotta shade, known as Pompeiian red, was based on the reds of antique Greek vases, which at the time were thought to be Etruscan. The so-called Etruscan rooms fashionable at the time were decorated with classical motifs picked out in Pompeiian red and black.)

Robert Adam was particularly known for his use of stucco decoration, often picked out in white to contrast with coloured walls, as seen in the Great Staircase of Kedleston Hall in Derbyshire. The staircase, which is top-lit, was finally finished in the 1920s to Adam's original designs.

Adam believed, as many of our top designers do today, that not only should the interior of a house be in sympathy with the exterior architecture, but also everything in the interior scheme should be as co-ordinated as possible. For this reason he designed all the furniture and furnishings to go with his rooms. His ideas even extended to placing paintings in stucco panels so that the frames would not clash with the scheme, and his carpets were specially made – sometimes to match the ceiling design.

His main reception rooms were always magnificent, though this was sometimes at the expense of other rooms in the house. Adam was also known for using a variety of room shapes, including circular, octagonal and square formats. His work mainly involved refurbishing existing houses rather than building new ones.

Towards the end of the century, the cult of the picturesque emerged, and began undermining neoclassicism. The complete opposite of the classical approach, this was full-blown romanticism. The style was adopted by the landowners for their country houses, resulting in a growing reaction against formality.

The picturesque style was responsible for the drawing room being brought down to earth, literally, so that French doors could open from it onto the garden. The symmetrical facades of neoclassicism were rejected in favour of asymmetrical floor plans, which were much more functional. Furniture was moved away from the walls to the centre of the room. The grand, formal country house had fallen from favour, and had been replaced by the smaller, more intimate country home.

This feeling that the main rooms of the house should be in touch with nature led to the rustic gradually being left out of new houses. Increasingly, the main rooms were at ground level, leading onto the garden or conservatory, and the bedrooms upstairs. The servants' and service rooms were housed in a separate wing.

The upshot of this was that the servants were often a long distance away when required. This led to the introduction of the bellrope and then later bell systems, so they could be summoned. Unfortunately, because of the significant distance between the kitchen and the dining room, food had to travel a long way down cold corridors, often resulting in unpleasantly tepid meals.

Staircases in late eighteenth century country houses were often gracefully curved. White marble was frequently used on the walls of the main rooms with a coloured marble inlay, but painted carved wood was a less expensive alternative. Wedgwood plaques were sometimes set into the marble, and ormolu (gilded bronze), bronze or gilding were also used as decoration.

Wainscoting featured much less on the walls now, and stucco was the most popular type of decoration, though used in lower relief. The chimneypiece, door and windows were often set in panels which were also used to frame paintings – a favourite technique of Robert Adam. Walls were usually painted in soft pastel shades or bright blue, green, turquoise, lilac or yellow. Wallpaper was also popular, particularly neoclassical designs.

The print room became fashionable during this period too. This was a method of decorating a closet, dressing room or study by pasting engravings on the walls and embellishing them with paper borders, chains and nails, cords, bows and festoons, also pasted straight onto the wall. The background colour was most often straw, but strong colours were also used.

Even floors might be grained or marbled, though parquet flooring was the norm in country houses. Wilton, Axminster

A charming print room effect, with the elongated black-and-white animal prints linked with a trompe l'oeil rope pasted onto both wall and door against a soft, neutral background.

The hall at Heveningham, Suffolk, is a perfect example of the cohesive style of the eighteenth century, with its inlaid marble and stone floor, scagliola columns and pilasters, detailed ceiling, white stucco, niches for statues and rich mahogany doors.

and Kidderminster (Brussels) fitted carpets, introduced in the 1730s and '40s, had become very fashionable.

Ceilings were now almost always of plaster, usually with a centrepiece, delicate decoration and a cornice. The background colours were pale, motifs were classically inspired and painted panels were smaller and more restrained than earlier in the century. Cornices were treated as wall mouldings, not as part of the ceiling.

The arrangement of furniture was changing as different activities now often took place in the same room at the same time. This meant that furniture had to adapt quickly for meals, card games, conversation or dancing. Folding tables were fashionable and the furniture layout was often more informal and placed more centrally in the room than before.

This was the finest period for English furniture. Mahogany was the principal wood,

but satinwood also became fashionable, and painted furniture with decorated panels in floral and festoon patterns was popular too. Well-known artists painted allegorical scenes on oval or circular panels on important furniture. Gilt was used a great deal, sometimes with paint for mirrors and picture frames. Scagliola (imitation marble) and Wedgwood panels and medallions were also often set into furniture. After Thomas Chippendale, George Hepplewhite and Thomas Sheraton were other great influences on furniture of the period.

Textiles were much lighter and less lavish now. Plain silks and cotton prints such as toile de Jouy had replaced velvets and brocades. At the beginning of the period, the first roller blinds appeared, in linen, silk or wire gauze.

Although light was still provided by candles, the level of illumination had been greatly improved by increasing the number of fittings used. A dazzling selection of chandeliers, candelabras, wall sconces and candlestands was used and the light they produced was then reflected in vast wall mirrors.

THE EARLY NINETEENTH CENTURY

By the Regency period, the newly wealthy middle classes had invested in land, built new houses and set up as landed gentry. Home was a symbol of stability and prosperity and much entertaining was done.

The changes to the country house layout that were begun at the end of the eighteenth century continued, resulting in smaller, less formal, more domesticated rooms. Conservatories became very popular now. On the whole, surfaces were plainer, and painted decoration replaced relief decoration. Motifs were Greco–Roman or Egyptian and included sphinxes, winged griffins, swans and the Greek key pattern.

The style of architecture fashionable during the Regency period was still predominantly Greek revival – having become fashionable in the 1780s, it reached its peak in the 1830s. The painted stucco facades were decorated with wrought iron balconies and bow or bay windows. Larger houses often still had porticos with columns and a flight of steps up to the front door.

White marble fireplaces were an important feature of the Regency drawing room, and were usually decorated with simple carving picked out with gilt or with painted or inlaid marble ornament. There was sometimes a mantelshelf or small projection, a decorative frieze and pilasters or carved figures.

The hall and kitchen floor were usually tiled at this time. The floors in other rooms were often polished wood covered with rugs or carpets. Brussels and Wilton close carpeting was still fashionable, and manufacturers produced a variety of beautiful carpet designs often with a centrepiece and outer border, or with floral or geometrical repeat patterns.

Nineteenth century ceilings, which consisted of plaster painted a light colour, were much plainer. Usually, the only decoration was a cornice decorated with classical motifs, or a central ceiling rose from which to suspend a chandelier. Papier mâché often replaced carving or stucco for cornice and frieze mouldings as it was considerably cheaper.

Walls were frequently painted in one flat colour, with strong colours, particularly crimson, often used for the dining room and library, and light colours used elsewhere. The palette was distinctive and exciting, including deep yellow, terracotta, cherry red, deep pink, vivid greens and rich blues and golds. Colour combinations were often strong, too, such as lilac with sulphur yellow, or crimson with emerald. Hand-painted or stencilled borders bearing Greek or

Egyptian motifs were often used, and marbleizing, graining, bronzing and cloud ceilings were all fashionable now.

Wallpaper was the most popular form of wallcovering now, and in the early part of the century it was light and bright and sometimes chosen to match the upholstery or curtains. It could be plain with a floral border or even with a satin ground and flocked. Stripes were rare – the so-called 'Regency stripe' was invented in the twentieth century. Hand-printed papers were still imported from China. Wallpaper usually covered the wall from wainscot to picture rail and the woodwork was painted in white or other pale colours to match the background of the paper. Stucco was now replaced with imitation marble.

Brocades, silks and chintzes were used for tented walls and ceilings. The tall, narrow windows of the Regency period were draped asymmetrically with multiple layers of curtains hung from elaborate poles. On top would be light-coloured silk, linen or chintz curtains. Contrasting under-curtains of silk or muslin were underneath, and below these there was probably a blind (shade) of some sort. The curtains would be caught back away from the window in order to let in as much light as possible.

Upholstery was mainly in silk, damask or brocade, which could be plain or striped or with delicately sprigged floral patterns. Chairs came in a mixture of shapes and styles, and seats could be of cane or wood with cushions or upholstery. Regency stools tended to be X-frame in mahogany or rosewood with a leather, cane or upholstered seat, but later stools were long and low, of carved mahogany with needlework tops. Light settees had cane seats and squab cushions with japanned (lacquered) frames. Grecian-style couches with curved rolled ends and short, outward curving legs ending in lion's paws were also fashionable.

Much of the furniture was rectangular in silhouette, with paw feet and dolphin, eagle or lion motifs. Rosewood and satinwood were used a great deal, though mahogany was still employed for larger items such as dining tables and bookcases. Cheaper furniture was made in beech or pine which could then be veneered, painted or japanned (lacquered). Faux bamboo was also very fashionable.

Furniture layouts were more homely and informal now, with the various pieces placed permanently in conversational groups away from the walls, and at angles to them. A large, round pedestal table frequently had pride of place in the centre of the room.

By the end of the 1830s, the beginning of the Victorian period, there were signs of Gothic influence once again. The main pieces of furniture in the dining room were massive, combined with a variety of smaller items. The drawing room was becoming overcrowded with a proliferation of small tables and work-tables, sofas, chairs and stools, china cabinets, piano, firescreens and decorative objects. Gothic vaulted ceilings were much admired, though most Gothic revival rooms had flat ceilings, with applied ribs and moulded beams to make them look vaulted.

Upholstery began to appear in darker colours, accented with paisley shawls used as throws, and petitpoint and embroidery. There was a fashion for needlepoint stools worked to match needlepoint rugs.

Candles were still the main source of light, though colza-oil lamps, designed to look like Grecian urns, came into use during the period. Wealthy homes would have expensive glass chandeliers with bronze or ormolu (gilded bronze) frames and myriads of exquisite cut-glass drops. These were supplemented with wall sconces, torchères (candlestands) and candlesticks. Candle-holders were made of brass, silver, bronze, iron, wood or porcelain.

In this enchanting Gothic-style saloon, in Birr Castle, Ireland, the fan-vaulted ceiling is white picked out in gilt and stands out against the damask-patterned handblocked wallpaper.

THE MID TO LATE NINETEENTH CENTURY

The Victorian era lasted till 1901 and, as a style period, was most notable for the number of style revivals it produced. Both the Greek and the Gothic revivals had become fashionable in the previous century, but the Gothic revival, which had begun to recede, became popular once more and overtook the Greek revival in the 1830s. Classical restraint gave way to medieval richness, and the Gothic revival steadily increased in popularity until the 1870s.

Other Victorian revivals included the Romanesque, Tudor, Renaissance (also known as Italianate or Beaux-Arts), Elizabethan, Louis XIV, Rococo (or Louis XV) and Louis XVI styles. In Scotland virtually all country houses built in this period were in the style known as Baronial. The Moorish style also had its followers.

Not only were most of these revivals inauthentic, but towards the end of the century it was not uncommon for several styles to be used in one house. Nevertheless, the majority of English architects turned to the traditional styles like Gothic, Tudor and Elizabethan. By the end of the century revivals of 'Queen Anne style', with Adam-style interiors, and 'Old English style' had replaced most of the previous fashions.

The principal change to the actual layout was the revival of the great hall. This had reappeared earlier in the century and from the 1830s became even more popular as part of the revival of the old traditions.

The new great halls, or 'living halls', were often quite different from the medieval or Elizabethan originals, however. Some, for example, were top-lit, which they never were in the Middle Ages, but they were especially good for the big house-parties that were popular at the time. They were built right through the nineteenth century and

The sturdy furniture and display of antlers in the hall of Kinloch Castle, Scotland, are typical of the Baronial style, which was particularly popular in Scotland in the mid nineteenth century. The mosaic floor with Moorish design is also characteristic of the period.

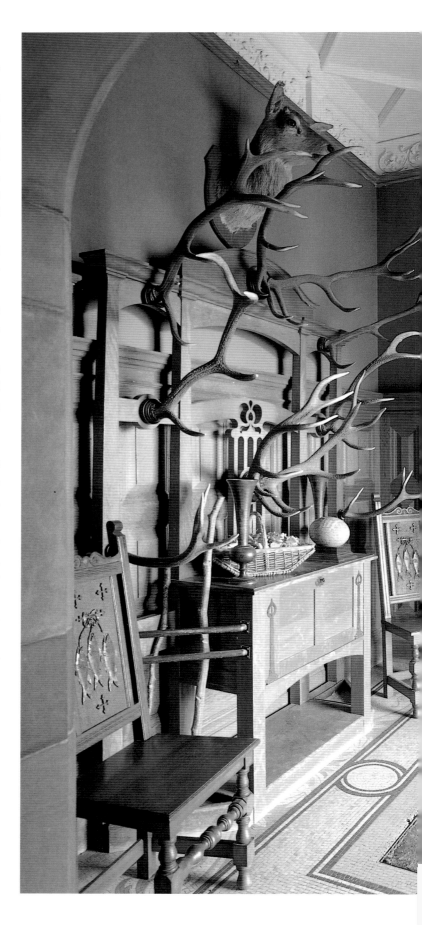

into the twentieth, becoming gradually more like informal living rooms, with increasingly low ceilings.

The drawing room and dining room were still much the same in terms of size and site. The dining room remained essentially a masculine room, with dark, heavy furniture, Oriental rugs and often a neo-Renaissance decor, while the drawing room had an inherently feminine feel, with gilt or rosewood furniture and soft furnishings in silk or chintz. One or other of these rooms often opened into the conservatory.

As the drawing room was more of a formal room than ever, informal life was confined to the morning room – which was used as a ladies' sitting room – and the library. The latter had become the principal informal living room, although its traditional role was now less important. It was particularly used as a sort of sitting room by the gentlemen.

Just as the ladies had a morning room, the men now had a smoking room. Although this had existed sporadically in the past, it did not re-emerge until the middle of the century. A ritual developed, which was for the men to retire to the smoking room with a tray of spirits after the women had gone to bed. Here they could combine the smoking of cigars with a game of billiards and risqué conversation. The decoration was often elaborate – Moorish style was a particular favourite. Another part of the male territory was the gun room, furnished as a sitting room but fitted with cupboards for guns.

The layout of the house became more complicated and often featured passages that went off in a number of different directions. In nineteenth century homes, the children of the family slept and studied above or next door to their parents. This family wing was the one vestige of the traditional apartment system to survive. The kitchen was still sited well away from the dining room – where it

was on another floor, a dumb-waiter (food lift) was frequently installed.

Houses were remodelled more than ever. However, most architects no longer designed furniture for the interiors of their houses so it was the upholsterer who acted as interior decorator and supplied all the necessary craftsmen and artisans. This meant that interiors were frequently more co-ordinated than before, but the schemes did not necessarily bear any relation to, or have any sympathy with, the interior architecture.

The colours of interiors varied according to the style, but in general the study, library and dining room were furnished in dark, rich colours , while the drawing room colours were lighter. Following the invention of synthetic dyes, colours became rather garish.

Although a few wealthy homes had installed rudimentary forms of central heating, coal remained the main fuel for heating well into the twentieth century. Most rooms were fitted with coal grates. In the living rooms, and also in the bedrooms of wealthy homes, fires would burn in these throughout the day during winter.

Lighting was provided by a mixture of candles, oil lamps – burning paraffin (kerosene) now – and gasoliers (gas-burning chandeliers, in which the flame burned upwards). The gas mantle, which allowed it to burn downwards, and electricity were introduced at the end of the century. Candles set in candlesticks continued to be used for dining. They were also used in wall, mirror and piano brackets and candelabra stands. Crystal fittings tended to be used in main rooms, and brass, copper or bronze was used elsewhere.

Staircases of the period tended to be dark and gloomy as the lighting was usually poor and dim. The woodwork was often dark brown – either natural or painted and grained – and the wallpaper dark crimson or green.

For most of this period the chimneypiece was a dominant part of the interior. Elaborately designed, it had a mantelpiece of black leaded or painted cast iron, marble or polished wood with scrolls, leaves, flowers or fruit. A Gothic version featured decorative arches surmounted by a mantelshelf, shelves, mirror and cupboard with a pediment and cornice. Towards the end of the century there was a return to Adam style, with classical mouldings and decoration. The surround and hearth would be tiled. Firescreens were used to cover the fireplace in the summer or curtains were drawn across it.

Kitchen, hall and conservatory floors were generally tiled, but in most rooms oak floorboards or parquet with Oriental or richly patterned rugs were used. Close carpeting was also a popular choice up until the 1880s, when it went out of fashion. At that time, there was a vogue for Brussels or Axminster squares within a polished oak surround. Matting was popular, too.

The ceilings were of plain plaster, whitewashed, distempered or painted in white or various pastel or neutral shades. The cornice and central rose were often quite ornate. In larger houses Lincrusta wallcovering was used to imitate eighteenth century plasterwork. There were also simple ribbed ceilings in the Adam style. The ceilings of some grand reception rooms were decorated with stencilled garlands of flowers and fruit, which sometimes extended down the walls if they were not already covered with wallpaper or fabric.

Walls were still usually divided into three sections. The frieze and infill (field) might be in dark patterned paper, perhaps in two different designs, though sometimes the frieze was taken in with the whitewashed ceiling. Wallpapers carried large motifs of flowers, fruit and birds in strong, rich colours such as Prussian blue, crimson and gold. The dado was usually plain plaster or

was painted in dark brown, grained to imitate wood or covered in Lincrusta. Woodwork was generally painted in a matt 'wood' shade or grained.

Tapestries and leather wallcoverings enjoyed a brief comeback, and paintings were hung together *en masse*. Different mediums and subject matter were all mixed together and could include prints, oils and watercolours.

Curtains or fabric covered virtually everything – not only windows, doors and beds, but even chimneybreasts and pianos. Lace curtains were used everywhere and portières were re-introduced for decorative purposes and to screen off draughts. Window treatments became symmetrical once more. The heavy curtains of mid-century gradually became lighter and fresher towards the end of the 1800s.

Furniture of the period was made from mahogany, walnut, oak or satinwood. Almost all was based on designs from earlier styles such as Jacobean or Georgian. All homes had a variety of cabinets and cupboards – china cabinets having glazed doors so that the best china could be put on display. One of the central features of the home was likely to be a grand or upright piano.

Seating was very varied and included chairs with plain wooden or cane seats, and button-back, balloon back or papier mâché chairs. There were many sofas and ottomans which usually had a mahogany frame and velvet or damask upholstery, decorated with embroidered beads and tasselled cushions. Settles were usually made of wood with either buttoned upholstery or squabs and were set into a corner by the fireside. Settees took the form of two or three chairbacks put together with cane seats.

Small round or oval tables were covered in cloths and ornaments. In fact, every available surface was covered with knick-knacks of some sort. Wall mirrors were used

The Great Parlour at Wightwick Manor, a Tudor revival country house in Staffordshire, is a fine example of an Arts and Crafts interior, with panelled walls, a settle in the inglenook, a frieze of roses and fabrics by William Morris and his colleagues. The Arts and Crafts movement embraced all things homespun and hand-crafted.

in nearly every room. Some would be very large with ornately carved gilded frames and others were of polished mahogany, oak or papier mâché.

In the last quarter of the century, the Arts and Crafts movement and the Aesthetic movement helped to make interiors lighter, simpler and more natural. Reacting against the clutter, garish colours and mass production of nineteenth century society, the Arts and Crafts movement, led by William Morris, advocated a return to hand-crafting in order to bring art to the working man. They substituted 'honest materials' like wood and exposed beams and floorboards, and stained glass for the ornate plasterwork and fussiness of Victorian colours.

Architects turned away from the styles of the Middle Ages and ancient Greece and Rome, and sought inspiration in vernacular architecture (using local crafts, skills and materials, including reclaimed bricks and tiles) and in Christopher Wren's late seventeenth century styles. These Queen Anne revival houses featured correspondingly lighter, simpler interiors. By the

close of the century attitudes in general were less extreme, and the country house lifestyle and decoration more relaxed.

THE EARLY TWENTIETH CENTURY

The image of the Edwardian country house is at least as evocative as any image from previous centuries. The creeper-clad, rambling old manor house, surrounded by rolling lawns and rose gardens, with the gentle sounds of croquet or tennis in the background, is for ever associated with the Edwardian period – that brief interlude between the Victorian era and the First World War.

As well as the genuinely old country houses that had become so delightfully mellow over the centuries, very similar-looking country houses were still being built as part of the Queen Anne revival. Sir Edwin Lutyens was the leading architect in this field.

The Edwardian country house incorporated most of the rooms found in its Victorian counterpart, including the drawing room, dining room, library and smoking room. The 'living hall', which had been revived in the nineteenth century, was still popular, though it was diminishing in size. However, the morning room, billiard room and conservatory were beginning to disappear.

The style of furnishing was now much the same as today's image of the country house. For the first time, there was considerable kudos in having furnishings that were frayed-round-the-edges. Antiques were highly sought-after, and reproduction furniture was now available to supplement them.

The country house aesthetic as we know it today was fully established by the beginning of the twentieth century, by which time the patina of time had acquired a new importance.

Rooms, and especially tabletops, were still cluttered, but there was no longer the claustrophobic feeling of the Victorian interiors. Pale-coloured walls and white- or cream-painted woodwork, combined with lighter fabrics and trimmings and fewer layers of fabric at the windows and on upholstery, made the rooms much lighter and airier.

The Adam-style decor that had become fashionable at the end of the Victorian era remained popular. Colour schemes included white and gold for the main reception rooms, and Wedgwood blue with off-white, lilac or grey.

Graining was now out of fashion, and walls sometimes had rectilinear panelling with plaster or wooden mouldings, which was then painted white or a pale colour. A feature of Art Nouveau-inspired interiors was the high wainscoting, up to one and a half metres (five feet), surmounted by a frieze bearing Art Nouveau motifs depicting stylized organic forms.

Walls that were not panelled were often painted. Papered or stencilled friezes were popular, too, and light, fresh wallpapers, particularly floral-patterned, and wallpaper borders were also used. In the hall, a painted embossed or relief paper such as Lincrusta would have been used below the chair rail. In other rooms, the chair rail had often been removed. Adam-style or Rococo-style decorative plasterwork was sometimes applied to friezes and chimneypieces.

Floors were most often polished woodblock or parquet, with Persian rugs, although tiles were used in the kitchen and hall. The main rooms might be close-carpeted with floral or plain carpets.

Armchairs and a sofa were grouped around the fireplace, and other chairs and occasional tables arranged in clusters. In keeping with the Adam revival, mahogany and satinwood Sheraton-style furniture was

The kitchen at Castle Drogo, designed by Sir Edwin Lutyens around 1910, included the latest labour-saving devices and was designed down to the smallest detail such as the chopping boards. The kitchen is top-lit, based on an idealized view of large medieval kitchens. The walls are local granite and the furniture limed oak.

particularly fashionable. Built-in furniture such as cupboards and seats in niches and inglenooks also became popular.

Table lamps were now the most characteristic lighting, many with frilly silk shades. Electric lights had been introduced, but most of the fittings looked like gaslight fittings or Adam-style wall brackets. Art Nouveau fittings were also used.

THE MID TO LATE TWENTIETH CENTURY

The twentieth century has seen many fashions in interiors come and go, but none of them has really affected the country house. However, the fashion for antiques, distressed wood, historically accurate wallpapers and faded, time-worn (or tea-dyed) fabrics has dominated the country house look. In fact, country house style might have remained frozen in an Edwardian time warp had it not been for a handful of interior designers.

Elsie de Wolfe, an untrained American designer and the pioneer of the profession, is generally credited with creating the 'period room' look. Inspired by English country houses on a visit to Britain in the 1880s, she furnished her American clients' homes with antiques – purchased on frequent buying trips to Europe – and the large-print chintzes that were her trademark. She painted the walls in restrained colours such as mushroom. From Elsie de Wolfe's period room look, the concept of country house style developed.

In Britain, society decorator Syrie Maugham and her rival Lady Sybil Colefax were the two most influential lady decorators of the 1930s. Syrie Maugham combined French antiques with modern Parisian furnishings, while Lady Colefax used chintz and quality English furniture to create traditional country house interiors. In 1938 she and the decorator John Fowler founded the decorating firm Colefax & Fowler, but after the Second World War she withdrew and the firm was acquired by the American heiress Nancy Lancaster.

Between them, Nancy Lancaster and John Fowler revitalized country house style and ensured its continued popularity. Most of Colefax & Fowler's work was in refurbishing country houses, many of which had become distinctly shabby. John Fowler

Geoffrey Bennison was a designer whose name will always be associated with country house style. This bedroom, with its canopied bed, is a good example of his work.

and Nancy Lancaster both had an affinity with country house style and were not overawed by it, so they were able to take the best aspects of the style and enhance them. Nancy Lancaster's style and panache and Fowler's brilliance helped them to achieve exactly the right effect, without being dull or predictable. The firm of Colefax & Fowler is still thriving today and is as closely associated with country house style as it ever was. Two of their leading designers in recent times were Roger Banks-Pye (who designed the hall shown on pages 4–5) and Chester Jones.

In the 1970s David Mlinaric developed a bolder version of John Fowler's style. Whereas Fowler's hallmark had been faded elegance, Mlinaric used an effective combination of apricot and mud colours, rush matting and linen upholstery. He utilized eclectic combinations of antiques and recreated period interiors using new textiles and gilding.

Similarly, the designer David Hicks expanded the look with more vivid colours, overscaled objects and geometric patterns. His work shows Baroque and Victorian influences, with crowded rooms, cluttered tablescapes and a brilliant mix of modern and antique furniture.

For many people the work of Geoffrey Bennison captured the quintessential English country house style, with faded and interestingly textured fabrics and fine antique furniture, to create a look that is still much sought after.

One of the most respected and influential figures in twentieth century interior design is Jean Munro of the company Mrs Munro. Her work on important country houses provides perfect examples of restrained and elegant country house style, with the emphasis on comfort.

Nina Campbell was one of John Fowler's protegées, and her stylish and comfortable interiors have been much admired in America and Britain for a long time.

Some of these designers are nearly household names, but the person who succeeded in making the country house style accessible to a vast number of people was Laura Ashley.

The Georgian style of country house has remained consistently popular for building. Existing country houses have been altered and refurbished to suit our current lifestyles, as they have through the centuries. It has become fashionable to convert outbuildings such as hunting lodges, follies

Country house style, as seen through the eyes of interior designers (such as Emily Todhunter, whose house this is), is a comfortable, easy-to-live-with look — traditional but with a modern twist.

and stable blocks into separate dwellings. Many of the big estates have been broken up, and as a result numerous country houses that were once the centres of those estates now have very little land attached to them.

The dramatic changes in lifestyle that have occurred since the First World War have had a major impact on the layout of the country house. Fewer bedrooms are needed now, but *en suite* bathrooms are almost *de rigueur*. Nowadays, the kitchen is the very heart of the house, and the study cum home office is frequently an essential. A playroom or den might be provided for the children, separate from the family sitting room. The formal drawing room that was only used for formal occasions is rare — it is somewhat alien to the culture of today to have rooms or possessions that are not fully used.

The decorative possibilities of ceilings have been well explored in recent years, not only by applying painted decoration such as trompe l'oeil cloud effects or rich colourings, but also by exploiting the actual roof structure. One way is to show the skeletal internal roof, while another is to create new architectural shapes, perhaps incorporating lighting schemes.

Cornices, where used, have tended to be simple and classical. Columns, pilasters, chair rails and other classical details have also been used to give definition and style to walls, and there has been renewed interest in the use of arches, niches and recesses. Tiles and wallpapers, often incorporating strong pattern, are much used today. The decorative possibilities of paint finishes and textured surfaces have been explored in great depth.

A wider range of flooring is available than ever before, but in country homes the traditional coverings still blend in best: wood floors such as parquet for reception rooms; quarry tiles for kitchens; tiles, terrazzo, marble, slate, granite or limestone in halls; and linoleum and vinyl for bathrooms.

Patterns are rectilinear and geometric, or historically based. There is also renewed interest in painted floor decoration such as stencilling. Patterned carpets have been revived, and sisal, coir and other natural floorcoverings are more popular than ever.

For many years, antique and good-quality reproduction hardwood furniture was the natural choice for the country home. But now modern pieces, sometimes specially commissioned, are often mixed in. There have been many exciting developments in the style and use of materials for bespoke furniture. Although many are quite contemporary in style, they can still work extremely well in traditional country houses.

As the trend continues for living spaces to become smaller and less cluttered, built-in furniture provides the ideal solution. Cupboards and bookcases are often given architectural detailing. Built-in kitchens come in a variety of woods and wood finishes or painted a flat colour or given a faux finish. However, there has been a move away from the fitted kitchen to the more individual freestanding kitchen.

The kitchen has become virtually the most important room in the house and often the one on which most money is spent. Some kitchens are very simple and minimalist whereas others are closely based on period style.

Country house style is still alive and flourishing, whether it is in an actual country dwelling or is a style applied to an urban home to give it a relaxing and escapist atmosphere. Although there are signs of its becoming a bit more pared-down, the style continues to adapt successfully to time and place. Chintz might now be replaced in favour of a gentle check or textured natural fabric, carpet give way to pale bleached wood floors and pictures and objects be displayed more sparingly, but the inherent qualities in the style remain.

American Country Houses

THE SEVENTEENTH CENTURY

Although it is clearly possible to trace English and other European influences in American Colonial architectural and interior styles, it developed its own distinctive qualities from the different nationalities that settled there and the importance of wood as a building material.

The earliest houses, which had a wooden frame covered with clapboards, were very simply laid out. The ground floor usually comprised two main rooms, a parlour or best room and the great hall or 'keeping room'. Both served as multi-purpose rooms, for living, eating and in some instances sleeping.

An enormous fireplace between the two rooms was used for cooking as well as heating. The kitchen was normally sited in a lean-to at the side, and the chambers above were for storage, with areas laid out in dormitory style for sleeping. They were reached by a narrow, winding stairway between the entranceway and the chimney-stack. The rooms were low-ceilinged, with exposed beams and unpainted or white-washed lath-and-plaster walls.

The houses that were closest to the English country house type were those of the tobacco planters in Virginia, which were small versions of the Jacobean manor. The Jacobean style persisted in the colonies long after the end of the period in Britain. These houses had panelled walls, beamed ceilings and coloured ornamental plasterwork, and the chimneys were at the ends of the house rather than in the centre.

The furniture in these Southern country houses and in the wealthier New England homes was Jacobean, imported from England. Homespun textiles were supplemented by imported damasks, velvets and other luxury weaves. They were used for bed hangings, rudimentary window curtains, table covers and seat pads.

THE EARLY TO MID EIGHTEENTH CENTURY

During this period, most grand country houses were found in Virginia and the South, among the plantation owners. English architectural influences were mainly introduced to America through published designs and pattern books. The Palladian style of Inigo Jones was clearly visible in the 'double-pile' houses, two storeys high, two rooms deep and five (or occasionally seven) sash windows wide. However, it was the late seventeenth century designs of Sir Christopher Wren which had the most marked effect on the Colonial style (the term for the style prevalent during the period until the Revolution in 1776).

The Baroque styling and classical proportions and detailing of Wren's designs were subtly interpreted in America. Although the houses varied in plan, they usually had a central door with a pediment on pilasters, heavy dormer windows, a balustrade and possibly a cupola. The hall was an important feature and the principal rooms were arranged symmetrically around this.

In the middle of the century, the designs of architects such as William Salmon and

Furnishings and decoration in Federal homes, such as Homewood House, Baltimore, built in 1801, were lighter and more elegant than those of the seventeenth century.

James Gibbs resulted in the appearance of the villa style of house with a very dominating central section, symmetrical wings and an open forecourt.

There were hardly any American architects at this time, so most houses were designed by the actual builders, who in turn were guided by their clients. Eventually the larger houses influenced the smaller homes. Sometimes these were built from scratch, but at other times, as in England, an existing building was given a new symmetrical Georgian-style facade and the interiors were updated.

In the early part of the century, the interior styles and finishes of country houses tended to be quite plain. By the second quarter of the century, the beams were completely concealed. Ceilings were of plaster with either a simple or carved cornice, though there were a few more elaborate versions inspired by German Baroque styles.

Floors were usually made of close-grained, wide, smooth pine boards without stain or varnish, though they might be stencilled. Stone floors were rare and most likely to be found in porches or halls, laid diagonally in a checked pattern. Some late eighteenth century floors might be painted in imitation stone. Parquet was found in wealthy homes, and some ground floors of country houses were brick.

Painted floorcloths were the most common form of floorcovering. Carpets were rare until after the Revolution and, if present at all, would be placed over a table. Rag rugs were common, and rush matting was occasionally laid over the floors.

Walls were plastered or part-panelled and then usually limewashed in matt white or a strong earth colour. Colours for interiors included an autumnal palette of yellow ochre, almond, blue grey, oxblood, deep green and brown, or alternatively very bright blues and greens. Some wood graining and marbleizing effects were used, especially in New England, and this also appeared on furniture such as tables and blanket cupboards. Blockprinted wallpapers and flocked papers appeared in some country houses at this time.

Locally made pieces of furniture were often simple but refined versions of English furniture, including rocking chairs, wooden armchairs, settles, slant-fronted desks and tallboys. The preferred wood was mahogany, but cherry, oak, birch, maple and walnut were all used, too.

Built-in furniture was an important part of American interior architecture. Designed to make the most of limited space, it could include shelved cupboards built into the fireplace wall, dressers, hanging cupboards and display cupboards divided into a lower storage area with display shelves above.

Candleholders included brass, pewter or wooden candlesticks, wrought iron chandeliers and iron wall sconces. Needlework items such as home-made samplers, patchwork quilts and rag rugs were widespread.

THE LATE EIGHTEENTH AND EARLY NINETEENTH CENTURIES

In the 1780s, following the American Revolution, there was inevitably a move to find an architectural style suitable for a new, independent nation. Neoclassicism, which had been fashionable in Europe since the 1760s, began to dominate smart American country houses from the late 1780s. Coinciding with the establishment of the new Federal government, the style-period became known as the Federal period. Thomas Jefferson's house, Monticello, which he designed himself at about this time, had a major influence on the development of Federal style.

Mount Vernon, shown here, was George Washington's family estate in Virginia. Originally a farm-house, it was his home for four decades. Washington based his design on Palladio's theories when he began enlarging Mount Vernon, but in the 1780s he adopted Robert Adam's neoclassical style.

(Right) The Federal style, America's interpretation of neoclassicism, was crisper and sharper-edged than the British version. Ayr Mount, a Federal-period home in North Carolina, shown here, has simple panelling and relies on ornaments and furniture to add decorative detail.

(Opposite) This bedroom at Ayr Mount, North Carolina, is decorated *en suite*, *with the pelmets and swags and tails at the windows designed to match the bed canopy, bedcover and upholstery. The only pattern is introduced into the ceiling of the canopy in the form of a red and white toile.*

Larger country houses started appearing north of Virginia from the middle of the century. Whereas the Southern houses were generally brick or stone, the Northern ones were most often timber interpretations of the brick country houses of Georgian England.

Characterized by grace and restraint, Federal interiors were generally lighter and more elegant than their Colonial-style predecessors. The rooms were more spacious, the ceilings higher and the detailing more intricate. As in Europe, the style was characterized by symmetry, clean lines and simple curves, but the designs, inspired by the work of Britain's Robert Adam, tended to be simpler, more severe versions of their European prototypes.

Decoration in particular was less ornate. Motifs, which were generally simplified versions of ancient Greek and Roman designs, included squares, circles, ovals, scrolling foliage, cornucopias, wheatsheafs, baskets of fruit, festoons, rosettes, urns, lyres, wreaths and columns. Also very popular were patriotic American symbols like the eagle, which was the symbol of ancient Rome and was also that of the new republic – notwithstanding Benjamin Franklin's preference for a turkey.

Interior architectural features became more sophisticated, with arches, smooth-running folding shutters, window seats and 'flying', or free-standing, staircases. Fireplaces were heavily influenced by Robert Adam, though the surrounds were generally of wood. The fireplaces were often supplemented by pot-bellied stoves.

In the grandest homes ceilings could be quite ornate, but lesser country houses generally had just a central plaster rose on the ceiling. Towards the end of the period, there were a variety of rich ceiling decorations, which ranged from complex geometric patterns to cloud effects complete with cherubs.

The furnishings and decoration of the smaller country houses were not as sophisticated as those of the townhouses of the same period, but many had a simple elegance that was just as appealing. A good example is this bedroom in late Federal style, with matching bedcovers in dark blue and white, and walls and bedsteads painted in a soft blue-grey.

The floors of the wealthiest homes might be of marble or stone, but most homes had hardwood or pine floorboards. Strips of carpet began to be used over the entire floor, and imported European or Oriental rugs were also fashionable in the wealthier homes. In less grand homes, painted floorcloths were still widely used, as they had been in the Colonial period.

Stencilled walls remained popular. Southern homes had very fine carved panelling, which was generally painted in a pale, soft colour. In the North it was used only on the chimneybreast or restricted to the dado, with smooth plaster painted in a light pastel colour elsewhere. Faux stone-work was fashionable for entrance halls and reception rooms.

Blockprinted wallpapers, bearing classical, 'architectural', geometric or possibly floral motifs, were sometimes used, often in conjunction with panelling. In the grandest homes, French 'scenic papers' were fashionable, even before they had caught on in England; these were hung either as panels or in sequence on all four walls of a room. The dining room was particularly favoured for this approach so that guests could dine surrounded by a classical panorama.

Coving, chair rails, skirting (baseboards) and other woodwork were often painted in deep green, blue, or soft, muted colours such as grey, mustard or deep violet. This contrasted with the light colours of the walls, which set off the rich colours of the soft furnishings, such as strong yellow, crimson or scarlet, rich blue and green.

Furnishing fabrics included wool or leather for upholstery, and imported printed cottons, chintz, silk brocades and damask for soft furnishings. Toile de Jouy was also imported, some of it printed with patriotic motifs relating to the Revolution. These fabrics were manufactured especially for the rapidly growing American market.

Window treatments became more formal, though not as elaborate as those favoured in Europe at the time. Restrained draped silk pelmets were fashionable, often trimmed with tassels and arranged into swags, perhaps asymmetrically. Curtains, when used, might be of translucent muslin, but often shutters sufficed. The popular canopy beds had restrained hangings in cotton, lace or crewelwork.

More elegant versions of the built-in furniture already so popular in Colonial-style homes were introduced, including built-in mirrors; break-fronted cabinets and cupboards in walnut, mahogany or painted or grained wood; and revolving doors, complete with shelves, connecting the dining room with the pantry.

Federal furniture was lighter, more rectangular and more finely carved than Colonial furniture and became one of the hallmarks of the style. Loosely based on designs by Hepplewhite and Sheraton, it was most often made from mahogany, but sometimes from rosewood, cherry, bird's eye maple or walnut. Painted furniture was popular too and was often decorated with gilt or japanning.

The dining room was a Federal-period innovation, and sideboards and extending dining tables were introduced for use in it. Shield-back chairs were common, and the Martha Washington chair — an upholstered chair with a high back and wooden arms, similar to the English Gainsborough chair — appeared at this time. Lambert Hitchcock's painted and gilded or stencilled chairs were particularly fashionable. From the beginning of the nineteenth century, the leading American furniture-maker was Duncan Phyfe.

Lighting was still by candles, which were used in chandeliers with glass drops and in candelabra that often had cut and engraved glass shades.

During the early part of the nineteenth century, America identified more with France than with England, and the 1820s were dominated by the heavier, more opulent Empire style.

The predominant architectural style during the 1820s–1850s was the Greek revival style. Although traditionally a Greek revival house is shaped like a classical temple, the American versions could be any shape. Interiors were fairly spartan, with simply moulded architraves and plaster walls, except for the parlour, which had a heavy cornice and other ornament.

THE MID TO LATE NINETEENTH CENTURY

As in England, this period was dominated by a plethora of style revivals, which were much the same as those in England. The Gothic revival followed hot on the heels of the Greek revival. American Gothic houses, built between 1840 and 1875, were the first American houses with an asymmetrical layout. The interiors were grand and stately, with lavish velvet hangings and curtains in deep colours like maroon or dark green.

Contemporary taste appreciated historic styles, often derived from Europe, combined with modern technological comforts and efficiency. The period interior detail was usually linked to the exterior architectural style, and interior styles by this time were running in parallel with those in England, and using many of the same published design sources.

A variety of styles were incorporated into the American vernacular during this period, including the Italianate style, also known as American Bracket, a so-called Second Rococo and a Second Empire, an Elizabethan revival, a Louis XVI revival known as neo-Grec, the Shingle style and the Stick style.

In America, the Beaux-Arts style was equivalent to the neo-Renaissance style that was popular in England and on the Continent. Very widespread, it was named after the École des Beaux-Arts in Paris, where many of the architects had trained.

Towards the end of the century a Queen Anne revival developed that was even more enthusiastically received than its English counterpart was. Furthermore, in 1876 the Centennial International Exhibition prompted a Colonial revival. This, combined with the Queen Anne revival, led to much lighter, airier interiors.

It was now possible to buy patterned papers for the ceiling with matching borders and central panels. In Beaux-Arts properties, ceilings would be designed to resemble architectural styles such as Tudor or Colonial – beams being a major feature of both. Stencilling provided another form of ceiling decoration, but by the end of the century, ceilings too were becoming lighter and simpler.

There were no dramatic changes in flooring, the most popular being unfinished, bleached pine boards, though it became fashionable to stain and polish these. Parquet was another popular option. Tiles were used for halls, and matting made of straw, coconut or cloth covered the wood floors in most other rooms, especially in summer, though they were sometimes replaced with rugs or carpets in the winter. Early in the century, floorcloths were used in kitchens, but these were gradually replaced by linoleum.

A much wider range of flooring and flooring designs was used in Beaux-Arts style houses where hall floors might have alternating black and white squares or lozenges, patterns of exotic coloured marbles or terrazzo tiles. In drawing rooms and dining rooms the parquet was often of oak with decorative borders in hardwoods such as cherry or mahogany.

With some styles, it was fashionable to paint the walls darker than the ceiling, but white or light-coloured walls were also popular. Faux stonework was still often used for halls, which tended to be decorated in sombre colours, so the drawing room or parlour would appear more warm and welcoming in contrast. Many wallpaper designs were inspired by nature, and organic patterns were also incorporated into friezes, which were used in conjunction with flat-painted walls.

In Beaux-Arts houses the walls of high-style classical reception rooms might have carved panelling with shallow relief ornament. The background could be painted white or possibly blue or green, and the mouldings and ornament picked out in gold. In Georgian revival homes the panelling would be plainer, while Colonial revival interiors combined panelled surfaces and smooth plaster, the only raised decoration being the chair rail.

Panelled dados usually appeared in dining rooms and halls, and in Tudor- or Jacobean-style houses this would be of stained oak often carved in complex patterns. Strapwork might also be used in interiors imitating this period. In very grand Beaux-Arts or Italianate mansions, marble slabs or limestone were used to set off magnificent antique tapestries.

Although furniture was, in the main, very similar to English furniture of the period, built-in furniture was a popular option in American interiors. There were many built-in cupboards and bookshelves, and benches and inglenooks were incorporated into fireplaces or window seats in Shingle and Colonial revival houses. Generously cushioned built-in seating known as 'cosy corners' was a frequent feature in sitting rooms, and built-in cabinets began to appear in kitchens, pantries and sewing rooms.

In Beaux-Arts style country homes, modern equipment was often adorned with delicate period detail such as acanthus leaves around the edges of brass switch plates, or cast iron dolphins on the feet of stoves and bathtubs.

Completely opposite to the Beaux-Arts style were the homes of the Shaker communities. Established in the late eighteenth century, the Shaker communities reached their peak in the mid 1800s. Their beliefs in superb craftsmanship, simplicity and clean, elegant lines are still influencing homes today, when the Shaker communities have all but died out.

THE TWENTIETH CENTURY

The Queen Anne revival that had begun at the end of the nineteenth century continued into the early twentieth century. In America as well as England, it featured asymmetrical layouts, more subdued colours and a new emphasis on antiques.

The Colonial revival, which also began in the late nineteenth century, led to the development of the Early American style. It is characterized by Colonial-style furniture, antiques and folk art, and fresh cotton fabrics like chintz, gingham, small-scale calico prints, plaids and stripes.

American taste was also influenced by country house style, which was subsequently adapted to meet the demand for a more polished look and more studied furniture arrangements. Often a mixture of the two styles is found in American country houses.

THE ENTRY HALL

DEVELOPMENT OF THE HALL

Over the centuries the hall has largely evolved from a general all-purpose living area to little more than a passage or a rectangular space giving access to other parts of the house. The very earliest halls had open hearths in the middle of the floor, which were used for cooking and heating, but by the fourteenth century fireplaces were beginning to be built into one of the outside walls. A very large hall would probably have had two such fireplaces. These usually had round arches and a flue cut into the wall which sent the smoke straight into the air immediately outside. This was not a very satisfactory system as the smoke often blew back in.

A typical fourteenth century 'great hall', as it was called, was two-storey and had a timber roof with exposed beams and lightly plastered stone walls hung with tapestries and rich cloths. The floor was tiled with stone slabs. The windows were made of stone decorated with tracery, with frames of lead, and panes, if used, of horn. The space was lit by candles in hanging wooden stands and metal holders in the walls. The furniture included chests in the window bays and large tables on substantial supports. Seating was mainly on stools; only the most important people had high seats, usually with carved backs and sides. Storage was in large cupboards secured with iron locks and bands.

As other rooms were gradually added to the country house, and the family began to live more and more in their private lodgings, away from the communal hall, the great hall became just a dining hall. In the first half of the sixteenth century the hall remained a double-storeyed large room with wooden 'screens' at one end to cut out draughts and a dais at the other. Walls were hung with tapestries or were oak-panelled, and the windows perpendicular in type, with a large bay or oriel window by the dais. Beyond the screens a passage led to the kitchen and buttery. The floor was of wood, left uncovered, and despite the large fireplaces the hall tended to be freezing cold in winter.

The hall had become smaller by the latter half of the sixteenth century. It was now often only one storey high, with a flat or pendant plaster ceiling. Decorative motifs in the plaster and woodwork included strapwork, semi-classical columns, various decorative figures, flowers and fruit. The woodwork itself was generally painted in bright colours, and the floor was usually flagged. The windows, though still in the simple Tudor style, were much larger than before and reached almost to the ground. Decoration was provided by arms and armour, stags' heads and flags hung on the walls.

By the mid seventeenth century the staircase had become the central glory of the house, often rising from the central hall

The staircase (which has been altered twice since it was built) is the central glory in the magnificent double-height hall at Chatsworth, Derbyshire. The painted ceiling, subdued colours and elaborate plasterwork are typical of seventeenth century interiors with Baroque influence.

to a galleried landing; a good example of this is the hall at Chatsworth, shown on page 49. As the century progressed the hall became smaller and less important, and by 1700 had become simply a large vestibule from which the stairs ascended. It still had a large fireplace with a chimneypiece above and a certain amount of furniture, especially chairs, a table, and a longcase clock. The floor was tiled or stone-flagged with a coloured rug in front of the fire.

The hall developed a new importance as an imposing entrance in the eighteenth century, especially in the grander houses, where the architects had often designed the interior details. However, in more modest country houses such as rectories and farmhouses, the sole purpose of the entrance hall was to provide adequate space to reach the stairs, which were usually at the rear to allow the principal rooms to have the best outlook.

The lighting was still by candles though in larger houses this might be supplemented by chandeliers, candelabra, wall sconces and candlestands of gilded wood and gesso or crystal. These were often accompanied by huge gilded mirrors to give a feeling of greater space and to maximize the candle-light by reflecting it.

A fine example of a nineteenth century revival of the great hall decorated in rich colours and a wonderfully eclectic mix of furniture and decorative objects. Mounted stags' heads were often displayed in these halls. A display of plates on the mantelpiece is typical of the period.

By the end of the eighteenth century the hall had again dwindled in size to become merely an entrance hall, though in some larger houses there was an outer entrance hall leading into the hall. Typical decoration included a plaster ceiling and frieze, low relief decoration in the Adam style, painted oval and circular panels, plaster walls and simple stucco decoration. The windows were sash, with wooden shutters or silk curtains. The hall had a tiled floor, in a black and white design, and polished mahogany doors. Lighting came from brass wall lights and carved and gilt wood chandeliers.

The nineteenth century country house entrance hall was usually square and was sometimes entered via an entrance porch divided from the hall itself by a stained glass and wood partition. Until the end of the century the decoration of the hall was distinctly gloomy. Woodwork was painted in dark brown, black or grained varnished paint. The walls were painted, wallpapered or covered with crimson, green or grey Lincrusta paper of a heavily patterned type, and also varnished. The ceiling and frieze were distempered, painted or papered, and patterned in dull tones.

The hall by the end of the century often resembled a mausoleum, as it was crammed with dark furniture, potted plants and ornaments, and was dimly lit by gas, oil lamps or sometimes candles. Large, solemn pictures obscured most of the remaining wall space, and the floor was tiled or of stone. It was occasionally covered with heavy oilcloth with designs in crude colours.

As part of the Gothic revival, the concept of the 'great hall' enjoyed a revival too during the nineteenth century. Like the example shown opposite, it tended to be a multi-purpose room that was used as a year-round living room, as well as for grander occasions such as balls. Sometimes it would house a billiards table or an organ, and it was frequently used for games, charades and amateur theatricals. It often included a staircase so that the descent of the ladies, after they had changed for dinner, could be admired by the assembled party.

By 1900 the decoration of the entrance hall had simplified a little, with fewer pieces of furniture, prints on the walls to replace large pictures and more adequate artificial lighting. The walls were still usually in a very dark colour, but the ceiling was a light distempered colour and the floor either dark stained oak or polished tiles with Oriental rugs.

In the 1930s, murals and trompe l'oeil work were used a great deal in halls and reception rooms. Often executed by talented artists such as Rex Whistler and Alan Walton, they brought new life to the interiors of country houses. As the twentieth century progressed, country house halls tended to become lighter and brighter and a place of welcome, reflecting the ambience of the house itself.

PLANNING THE HALL

The entrance hall provides an introduction to your home. It makes the first impression, setting the tone for everything beyond and will be all the more welcoming if it is planned and decorated as a room rather than a passage.

Many older country houses were built with spacious, well-proportioned halls which were often used as a form of reception room as well as serving as an arrival and departure point and providing access to the rest of the house. It was often customary in country houses in the Southern states of America to place an elegant sideboard in the hall from where refreshment would be offered at various times of the day. In many English country houses afternoon tea would be laid out in the hall.

Space has been maximized in this hall with the addition of a desk and chair to create a valuable working space. The decoration is simple and restrained, with cream walls and upholstery and with touches of rich colour in the leather top of the desk and the patterned runner on the stone floor.

Using the hall in this way not only makes it a more inviting room but also effectively adds to the usable space in the house. A similar idea would be to add a desk, as in the hall shown in the photograph above, and perhaps some bookshelves, so that it could also operate as a study or library. Even a small hall could be adapted in such a way and would create an ambience very like that in a working country house.

HARD-WEARING FLOORING

The hall also acts as a connecting area to rooms on the same floor, as well as to the staircase. Even when there is a back door to take the worst of the incoming and outgoing traffic, the hall is likely to take a great deal of wear and tear, and so the floorcovering in particular needs to be hard-wearing and practical.

These days, there is a huge range of flooring to choose from. Materials that are indigenous to a particular region always look in keeping and most forms of hard flooring are a practical choice for a hall. In sixteenth, seventeenth and eighteenth century houses local stones such as York, granite, slate and marble were often used. Brick was used too, but it tends to disintegrate with heavy wear and tear so is not really suitable.

Flagstones are often found in period homes and are ideal for halls and entrances. They are available in large oblongs or squares and come in a range of pleasing neutral colours. Slate is another very suitable choice, particularly as it can be given a special non-slip finish. It varies in colour depending on where it is quarried and can be found in greys, greens and blues.

In a well-proportioned hall an effective decorative device is to incorporate a central motif into the floor design. During the seventeenth and eighteenth centuries, increasingly elaborate patterns were introduced, often with inlaid marble work. Portland stone was a popular choice laid in a diamond pattern intersected with small squares of black marble.

Tiled floors were also found in many nineteenth and early twentieth century halls. Made up of encaustic tiles (see page 185) mixed with plain-coloured tiles in different shapes and sizes which were known as 'geometrics', they were laid in intricate geometric patterns. This type of tile is still available today (at a price).

In Victorian and Edwardian halls quarry tiles were laid with interestingly designed border patterns. They are very tough and frostproof, but need sealing as they are porous. Wall to wall carpet would have to be very carefully chosen as it tends to have a fairly urban feel and the colour would be an important consideration for practical reasons.

A mat well is a good idea for any country hall. In a fairly rustic scheme, natural floorcoverings such as coir or sisal (see page 81) will blend in well and are reminiscent of the rushes and rush matting that would originally have been used in the great hall.

Natural floorings can 'move' and be slippery underfoot, however, so should be avoided on stairs or in a household with elderly people. The hall flooring does not, of course, have to match the stairs and landing, though an unbroken finish can increase the sense of space. It is important, however, to keep some link in colour or design not only with the hall floor and the staircase, but with rooms opening off the hall which might be seen when the doors are open.

WELCOMING COLOUR SCHEMES

Colour has a vital role to play in the hall. Not only can it help to create a warm and welcoming atmosphere and set the mood of the whole house, but it can also be used to correct awkward shapes and increase or reduce the impression of space as required.

The most conventional starting point for a colour scheme is the floorcovering, but almost anything could provide the spark of inspiration, from a painting to a piece of pottery. In a period house or a period-style decor, the colour scheme might be linked to the architectural style of the house, incorporating colours associated with a particular period. For example, the green of the walls in the photograph below was

The strong green used on the walls of Homewood House, Baltimore, is typical of the eighteenth century, when this country house was built. The fresh, white woodwork, and subtle, soft green detailing of the magnificent fanlights, the pilasters and the chair rail enhance the green. The whole treatment is very much in keeping with the architecture.

The plain floorboards and cream walls in this hall will not conflict with the decoration of any of the rooms it leads to. The stencils of fruit trees in Oriental ceramic pots on either side of the front door provide the main decorative element.

typical of the eighteenth century, when this house was built. In an old house it is sometimes possible to scrape back the paint with a coin to try to find an original colour under the layers.

Many very well-researched ranges of historical paint colours are now available, enabling you to choose colours that would actually have been used during the particular period you have chosen for your decor.

When choosing your colour scheme, be sure to take into account the schemes of adjacent rooms. The hall provides a link between rooms not only physically but also visually. It is at the centre of your decorating scheme, helping to pull it all together.

Neutral colour schemes are a safe choice as these will not fight with the colour schemes in adjacent rooms and will give a general

The pine panelling in this hall has been painted in a subtle aqua-blue which enhances the gilt frames of the paintings, an effect reminiscent of early eighteenth century paint effects. The colour works well with the stone floor and antique upholstery.

A soft, warm and welcoming colour scheme in this hall, with apricot walls, terracotta tiles and an Oriental rug softly patterned in rust, blue and gold.

feeling of cohesion. They also provide the perfect background against which to display striking furniture, pictures and decorative objects – or even stencilled motifs, as in the photograph on page 54 – in order to create an impact as you enter the house.

Neutral schemes, however, can be just plain dull if not enhanced by the use of different shades, textural contrasts and accents. Also bear in mind that light colours will show up fingerprints and marks, particularly on the lower parts of the walls.

A strong colour scheme can be very dramatic but could limit your options in adjoining rooms. Nevertheless, in a large hall with dominant architectural features, where substantial paintings or sculptures might be displayed, a strong colour such as a deep yellow, various shades of terracotta or even a rich blue could look magnificent.

Vivid colour like this looks particularly effective where plaster or stucco work is picked out in white in complete contrast. This was a technique frequently used by Robert Adam in the eighteenth century.

In the early eighteenth century, plastered or pine-panelled walls were mainly painted in muted tones such as white, stone, drab or olive, with the mouldings picked out in gilt. The use of soft, muted tones with gilt could make a sophisticated and appropriate scheme for a hall today, as illustrated by the hall on pages 54–5. It will still leave maximum scope for the colour schemes in reception rooms beyond.

Vertical patterns on wallpapers or other materials will give an impression of more height. Flooring with a well-defined linear pattern will make a room look wider if the direction of the pattern is used across the narrowest part of the room, and fitted carpet also increases the impression of floor space. If the skirting is painted to match the floor, this again will make the hall look larger. Tiles laid from corner to corner have a similar effect by drawing the eye to the pattern.

The use of strong colour on the lower part of the walls, though reducing the apparent height of a room, will, at the same time, make a narrow hall look wider. Another way of achieving this is the use of horizontal line effects either in pattern or materials. Avoid juxtaposing a strong, dark ceiling colour with light coloured walls, which would make the room seem lower and narrower.

Think about the direction the windows face and the amount of natural light entering the hall, before making a final colour selection. A north- or west-facing hall, dependent on natural light during the day, will benefit from a warm colour palette such as soft pink or apricot. By contrast, a south-facing room could look wonderful decorated in cooler colours such as pale blue or green, while an east-facing room would glow in the morning light if the walls were in yellow or ochre. Also, a scheme based on cool, pale colours will increase the sense of space and so would be useful in a small entrance hall. A hall that seems cold can be pulled together by the emphatic use of one warm colour, perhaps taken from a painting that is hanging in the room and then reproduced in rich curtains, some upholstery and an elegantly faded rug on the floor.

PRACTICAL WALLCOVERINGS

For maximum impact, a decorative paint effect in the hall is a good choice. Woodgraining and faux stonework (see pages 100 and 137) are both particularly suitable. Not only are the materials they imitate found in country houses but the actual paint effects have been used in these houses too for centuries. For a really subtle finish, however, they should ideally be applied by a specialist.

In a very dark hall a broken finish, such as ragging or stippling, introduces more light and tends to make the space look bigger. A paint with a sheen will also help make the most of any light there is, but it will show up unevenness on a surface as well, so if your walls are not in ideal condition, a matt finish would be a better choice.

Apart from all the standard colours, further variations can be produced by the so-called tinting system, where paints are specially mixed by the supplier. A number of specialist companies make up paint to order and many companies offer a historical range of colours. The paint charts show a mouth-watering range of colours.

One of the most popular decorative paint effects for halls in recent years is 'stonewalling', which provides a neutral background with texture and interest. In this Gothic revival interior it rises from the hall up through the staircase walls to the top of the house.

RELIEF WORK

The first high-relief wallcovering, Lincrusta, was introduced in the late nineteenth century. It was followed by Anaglypta, a lighter-weight embossed paper. Both were used on friezes (the areas above picture rails) and dados (wainscoting) and also over the entire wall. The hallway and staircase were the most popular sites for these wallcoverings, which were always painted. A limited range of Lincrusta patterns has recently been re-introduced, while Anaglypta has been in continuous production.

A patterned wallpaper can hide the inevitable marks and scrapes caused by suitcases, brooms, mobile toys and the like. The Victorians favoured heavily textured wallcoverings as they were virtually indestructible and could be produced to imitate timber panelling, stamped leather or plaster relief work.

SUITABLE LIGHTING

Because the hall is often just seen as a link with the other rooms in the house, rather than an entity in its own right, lighting here is often not given sufficient attention. This casual attitude can result in a couple of ill-placed wall lights and an unsuitable central pendant. The lighting needs to be functional as well as decorative and to create a

Atmospheric pools of light from table lamps link this hall with an adjacent sitting room, leading the eye from one room to the other and creating a warm, welcoming glow.

welcoming atmosphere while still having careful regard for safety. Electrical work has to be done very early in a job, so it's important to plan your lighting scheme at the outset. It helps to break it down into the three main types of lighting that are needed in a room.

The first type is general lighting, also known as ambient lighting, which provides a good general illumination. In the hall, general light could be supplied by downlighters recessed into the ceiling, a central pendant or lantern, wall lights or wall-mounted uplighters. Floor-mounted uplighters can give a very strong light but are not really in keeping with country house style.

Second, task lighting, sometimes called work lighting, will be needed if any particular function is carried out in the hall. For example, if the hall doubles as a study then the desk will certainly need some form of task lighting. This is usually provided by lamps.

Third, and equally important, there is decorative lighting, which will add drama and interest to the hall. It could perhaps be in the form of an attractive table lamp on a consul table to create a pool of light. Another idea is to highlight decorative objects using picture lights, or a flower arrangement using directional downlighters. If the space below the stairs is not needed for storage, an interesting piece of furniture could be positioned in the recess, and whatever is displayed on it highlighted. In a long, narrow hall, pools of light from downlighters or wallwashers reduce the feeling of length and make one feel drawn along the space.

MODERN LIGHTING IN THE COUNTRY HOUSE

Modern high-tech lighting can usefully supplement more traditional forms of lighting like chandeliers, wall sconces and table lamps in a country house style home.

Downlighters shine light downwards from the ceiling, where they are usually recessed or semi-recessed into holes. They come in different sizes, with broad, medium or tight beams. Basic ones take reflector bulbs, while more deluxe versions are fitted with silver or gold integral reflectors. The mellow, warm glow of gold makes this type especially well suited to country house style.

Eyeball fittings are downlighters with a rounded base that can be swivelled.

Low-voltage downlighters have a transformer built in or concealed in the ceiling. The bulbs are smaller than conventional types and give out a clean white light.

Wallwashers are a type of downlighter that casts light down the walls of the room. Mounted on the ceiling or a track, they are spaced about a metre (a yard) apart. Wallwashers are useful for emphasizing architectural features, wall textures and picture displays. These too can be mains or low-voltage and can provide a tight beam or light the wall evenly.

Uplighters beam light up towards the ceiling. They come in various forms, including small floor lights, tall standard lamps and wall lights. Small uplighter bulbs can be hidden behind cornicing or in the tops of cupboards.

Stairs obviously need to be well lit for safety, but the lighting can also be placed so as to emphasize any interesting architectural details. Ideally, the top and bottom steps should be lit and the fitting(s) placed so that there is no light shining directly into anyone's eyes. Not only is glare unpleasant and potentially hazardous, but it is also completely out of keeping with the atmosphere of a country house. Wall lights following the line of the stairs will give good general light but need to be at the right height to bounce light off the ceiling above, without giving out any glare.

Stair lighting could be put on a timer which switches it on automatically as the daylight fades, and on dimmer switches so that it can be turned down to a very low setting at bedtime to provide low-level lighting at night. There should be light switches at the top and bottom of the stairs. On landings where there is a change of level, the step could be emphasized with a downlighter.

The style of the actual light fittings is an important element of the scheme and should be in harmony with the overall effect. For example, Dutch bowl wall brackets would be an appropriate choice for a late seventeenth century style hall, while ornate Rococo-style fittings or elegant neoclassical ones would suit eighteenth century schemes.

DOOR AND WINDOW TREATMENTS

An attractive way of keeping out draughts is the portière, which is a curtain hung directly across the front door or an arch. Often used in country house halls, the portière is frequently designed to open with the door. A functional alternative is a tall, decorative screen.

Window treatments, if required, should fit the general mood of the hall. Paired curtains with crescent or rope tiebacks, hung from a pole as in the photograph on the left or from a simple pelmet, would be in keeping with the style. The aim is to soften the architecture without dominating the area as a whole.

In a dark hall a fabric with some sheen would help to reflect extra light, while a rough-textured fabric could look marvellous contrasting with a smooth, shiny floor. Hall furniture tends to be quite 'hard-edged' so a soft window treatment can be used to offset this.

Curtains that trail on the floor can look very elegant in high-ceilinged rooms and will also help to cut out draughts, but are very vulnerable in an area with so much through traffic.

As with pale walls, light-coloured fabrics, especially unpatterned ones, will attract dirty finger marks, mud splatters and possibly the artistic efforts of small children. A relatively bold pattern is therefore a more practical alternative.

Simple and elegant pole-hung French-pleated curtains complement this Gothic-style window rather than over-whelming it. They have been made up in a pretty small print with tiebacks and bordered in pink and brown for definition and interest.

FURNITURE FOR LARGE OR SMALL SPACES

In a large hall, like the one on the left, a circular table placed in the centre of the room makes a good focal point, whether it is an antique drum table holding a splendid flower arrangement, or a chipboard (particleboard) table covered with rich fabric and piled with inviting books. Antique fabric in a tablecloth or cushion, however small the piece, provides an excellent way to suggest the warmth and richness of country house furnishings.

Alternatively, the symmetry of a pair of consul tables adds form to the area. Even if you don't have room for either of these options, at least one table is invaluable in a hall for leaving keys, notes and other paraphernalia.

A chair for someone to sit on while waiting or when removing boots is useful, and a longcase clock is not only decorative and practical but also introduces a valuable element of height into the space (not to mention a reassuring ticking).

An interestingly shaped hall may provide the perfect opportunity to create an attractive display area for ornaments or books. Areas next to pipes that have been boxed in are often ideal for this purpose, and carefully placed lighting can add drama and interest. A hall is not an obvious place for displays of china or books, but either can make an attractive and welcoming feature.

Storage is usually an important consideration. Guests' coats and hats will almost certainly need to be hung in the hall

A circular table covered in a rich black-and-gold fabric with a deep bullion fringe makes a splendid focal point in this hall. Piles of books, casually placed ornaments and an informal arrangement of summer flowers add a relaxed and hospitable touch.

In this hall there has been no attempt to hide away coats, hats, sports gear and shoe-cleaning equipment. Instead, they have been made an integral part of the decorative display.

or adjacent to it. If there is no rear entrance to the house, boots, jackets and sports equipment may also need to be housed. It may be that the recess under the stairs is the only place where these can be stored, especially if the cluttered look of a coatstand does not appeal. Sometimes a simple row of pegs is all that is needed, as in the hall shown above.

As the hall provides the first view the visitor has of the house, and therefore the ideal opportunity to indulge in a little impact and drama, it is the perfect place to try out a mixture of ancient and modern. The designer David Hicks (see page 35) has been one of the great exponents of this style of decoration, successfully combining his own customized furniture designs and modern materials with classical eighteenth century furniture and ornamentation.

One way of achieving this is to combine decorative objects of different periods and styles but of the same material. Another approach is to aim for total contrast – for example, a modern abstract painting mounted above an ornate eighteenth century consul table. An antique chair could be upholstered in a vibrant modern fabric. Primitive art could be juxtaposed with eighteenth century furniture, or bleached driftwood and stones set against an unframed modern picture, or panelling used to frame interesting modern paintings.

Though not so closely associated with country house style as traditional furnishings, this approach is fundamentally consistent with it, since country houses have always been noted for their eclectic, highly personal combinations of furnishings and ornaments.

PICTURE GALLERY

The stairwell is usually the largest expanse of wall space in a house and so offers the perfect spot for a picture gallery, as the photograph on the left demonstrates. The pictures in a group need to relate to one another in some way, whether they are similarly framed or linked by subject matter. However, it's equally important for them not to be too similar, or the grouping will become monotonous.

The arrangement will need careful thought so the pictures don't look as though they have arrived there by accident. The easiest approach is to try out various layouts on the floor before attempting to hang the pictures on the wall.

A gilt-framed group of watercolours makes a pleasing display on the walls of this staircase. The four pictures at the base of the stairs are effectively hung within the wallpaper border.

The classical severity of this elegant hall is nicely offset by the bust (complete with hat) and vase of flowers. Anything else would be superfluous.

The strongest pictures should be placed above centre in the group, but there are various shapes around which you can base the arrangement. One way is for the pictures all to be in a row, appearing either to stand or to hang from an imaginary horizontal line. Or they can be arranged symmetrically on each side of a vertical line.

You could have two rows of pictures, the lower one hanging from the line and the top one sitting on it. In addition, if desired, the pictures could also be arranged symmetrically around a vertical line down the middle of the horizontal one.

Another idea is to place the largest pictures at the corners of an imaginary rectangle, with smaller ones touching the edges of the rectangle or filling in spaces between the others. With an even number of pictures of the same size, the best arrangement is often simply to arrange them in equal-sized rows, placing them equal distances apart within the block.

One more approach is to arrange them within a triangle or an inverted triangle, with the smallest pictures near the point. (This is also a good way of making a ceiling appear higher.)

ACCESSORIES FOR THE HALL

A mirror always adds depth and interest to a room and is almost obligatory in a hall. It should ideally be framed in keeping with the architectural style of the hall, like the mirror in the photograph on page 64. Old mirror glass, or antiqued glass, is more suitable than new glass, which can look harsh. Placing it opposite a window looking out onto the garden will give the impression of bringing the garden into the room.

Plants and flowers offer the most natural and appropriate decorative accessory for a country house style entrance hall. In a small, informal country house style home, unusual containers such as soup tureens and teapots can look charming. Huge baskets of casually arranged plants or flowers are quite in keeping with the overall style of such a home. For a hall in a larger, more formal style of house, neoclassical urns and elegant planters with formal arrangements would be more suitable. In a high-ceilinged hall, tall floor-standing plants in formal containers will look striking. They could even be highlighted with strategically placed lighting.

FLORAL BOUQUETS

A country house is incomplete without a wonderful, fragrant, freshly picked bouquet on the hall table. In keeping with the general ethos of unstudied elegance, the most typical arrangements are those which look as though huge armfuls of blooms have been casually jammed into the nearest (antique porcelain) vase. In reality, a lot more care usually goes into the arrangements. However, the type of bouquet that fits into country house style best tends not to be a stylized and artistic arrangement of florist's material. Instead, it is simply a large and informal bouquet containing an abundance of garden flowers, foliage, berries and branches that reflect the changing seasons. These arrangements are an essential part of the style, and creating them is one of the great pleasures of country house life.

THE SITTING ROOM

The first forms of sitting room in early country houses were a million miles away from the relaxed, comfortable, well-heated sitting rooms of today. To begin with, there were no separate sitting rooms as such, because the great hall was a multi-purpose area for living, dining and sleeping.

However, parlours – from the French *parler*, to talk – situated on the ground floor usually, had appeared by the end of the fourteenth century. The parlour provided a more intimate space which was generally used as an informal sitting and eating room for the owner of the house and his family. Sometimes these had beds, but by the beginning of the sixteenth century, parlours had become more important and the beds had disappeared from them in larger houses, which often had several parlours.

The 'withdrawing room' was another room with a similar function. During the sixteenth and early seventeenth centuries, it was sited between the great chamber and a bedchamber, and was still associated with bedchambers even in the eighteenth century. Gradually, though, from the seventeenth century onwards, withdrawing rooms not connected to bedchambers began to appear.

By the end of the sixteenth century, formal dining took place in the great chamber (sometimes called the great dining chamber) rather than in either the hall or the withdrawing chamber; informal meals however, were still eaten in the parlour. Comfort became an increasingly important element in the withdrawing room. Decorative hangings were introduced to keep out draughts, and seats were softened with cushions. Now that windows had increased in size, the interiors were generally less gloomy, and shutters and early forms of curtaining contributed to the cosy effect. The parlour was becoming more important too, and was sometimes called the 'great parlour' or the 'dining parlour'.

The withdrawing room took on a much grander character in the seventeenth century. No longer associated with a private bedchamber, it became more of a general reception room, and the furniture was more varied and richly decorated. It was still smaller than the great dining chamber, off of which it led. At this time these two rooms were still upstairs, but now centrally placed, and the parlour was underneath them. By the end of the century, however, they were both increasingly sited downstairs.

An eighteenth century formal country house would probably have had several reception rooms which, apart from the dining room, included a drawing room, at least one parlour and perhaps a card room. The prevailing fashion at that time was to site them

An example of the lighter interiors fashionable at the end of the eighteenth century. Furniture arrangements were more informal and relaxed and encouraged conversation. The gilt-framed furniture with upholstery in pale figured silk was typical of the period.

The drawing room at Standen, West Sussex, with wallpaper and carpet designed by William Morris and his colleagues. Although drawing rooms were still used as formal rooms at the end of the nineteenth century, there was a considerable emphasis on comfort.

all on the first floor. At this stage, the drawing room was used as a room to which the ladies withdrew, to gossip and brew tea or coffee after a meal. Because ladies and gentlemen spent such long periods on their own in the drawing and dining rooms respectively, the drawing room became thought of as a mainly feminine room, and the dining room as a masculine one.

By the end of the eighteenth century, the main floor was on the ground once more. The drawing room and parlour were therefore sited there again, with French doors opening out onto the garden. Furniture was arranged in a more informal way, as illustrated in the photograph on page 67, with chairs and sofas placed so they no longer hugged the walls. Smaller country houses had just one drawing room or sitting room. However, in the larger country houses

the dressing room of the lady of the house was still furnished as a sitting room and her female guests often spent the morning there. Similarly, her husband often used his study as a secondary sitting room.

During the heyday of the country house weekend party, the mid nineteenth century, guests were expected to spend a large part of their days downstairs in the reception rooms when not involved with sporting activities. The degree of comfort and detail in the drawing room reflected this.

The drawing room was not replaced by the great hall when the latter was revived in the nineteenth century. Still furnished in a feminine style, with delicate gilt or rosewood furniture and curtains and upholstery in silk or chintz, the drawing room was used for two particular functions – morning calls and afternoon tea.

This unusual interpretation of the print room idea (see pages 23 and 24), with charming groupings of differently shaped prints on either side of the fireplace, calls attention to the focal point of the room — the fireplace.

When afternoon tea was first introduced it was usually served to ladies in the boudoir, but by the turn of the century it had become firmly established as one of the major institutions of country house life. Indeed, both sexes took an elaborate tea in the drawing room unless the weather was fine enough for it to be served in the garden. As a result, the drawing room remained a formal room, and informal life was confined to the morning room, the library or possibly the great hall.

Since the beginning of the twentieth century, as our lifestyles have become more informal, the drawing room has gradually become less formal and has turned into the sitting room. The idea of having a room set aside for formal use seems old-fashioned now and is mainly confined to the grander country houses. Although it may be supplemented by rooms for other purposes, in most homes there is one sitting room providing a comfortable environment for all occasions.

PLANNING THE SITTING ROOM

Country house style is a unique blend of formal and informal elements, and nowhere more so than in the sitting room. Generous proportions, large windows framing leafy views, an open fire in the hearth, softly faded textiles, polished wood and an eclectic assortment of family heirlooms and memorabilia all make the country house sitting room simultaneously gracious and comfortable, elegant and unpretentious.

When planning the layout of the room, start with a focal point that people can sit around, and then work outwards from that. The fireplace is the obvious choice — indeed, 'focus' is Latin for 'hearth' or 'fireplace'. The designer Nancy Lancaster (see page 34) often referred to three essential elements in her decoration: wood fires, real candlelight and fresh flowers. An open fire is the ideal here, though a log- or coal-effect gas fire is a labour-saving alternative that can

This highly decorative screen painted with a rural scene discreetly hides a service area with a drinks table. A screen is a useful way of introducing height into a room to balance other tall pieces or a high ceiling and can also act as a room divider.

look surprisingly realistic. If the existing fireplace is not in keeping with the architecture of the room, it could be replaced with a more appropriate style. Architectural salvage yards have good selections of old fireplaces, and there are also many reproduction styles. The seating arrangement shown in the photograph on page 69 is one of the most popular.

In a room that doesn't have a fireplace, a window with a nice view could be the focal point. If the television has inadvertently become the focal point, an attractive cabinet

would help it to blend in with the decor (see page 87). Or place it in front of an interesting bookcase.

An area that seats more than eight can seem overwhelming, so, if space allows, it is better to create one or two other semi-independent seating areas within the room. Chairs and sofas should be arranged to 'talk'

to one another, without being completely cut off from other groups. They should also look as though they can be moved wherever one wants. And there should always be somewhere to put down a drink (see page 87 for suggestions).

Although three-seater sofas are well-suited to large rooms, they are best used for seating two people in comfort. Very seldom will three people actually sit in a row, as it is difficult to converse.

A sitting room needs to fulfil a variety of functions, all generally requiring furniture of some sort. A table may be needed for cards or other games; a television, video and music system may need to be housed; collections may be displayed and a small desk is often necessary. The number of people the room has to seat is obviously important too, and the lighting will need to be carefully related to the activities in the room. For example, a special reading area with appropriate lighting might provide a welcome retreat.

The room will be much more comfortable to live in if there is a good flow around it. Where the furniture is placed can make a great deal of difference, and sometimes a small structural change such as rehanging the door so it opens the other way or widening the doorway to take double doors or even re-siting the entrance can greatly improve the layout. This feeling of movement in a room is important and if any one element within the scheme is too dominant it can catch the eye unnecessarily and break the feeling of harmony.

If the room is to be dual-purpose, the division could be designated by a table of some sort with an attractive display of books or flowers. A handsome screen, such as that shown in the photograph above left, could also be used to separate the areas. This concept works particularly well in a long, narrow or L-shaped sitting room.

MELLOW COLOURS

Take into account the amount of light the sitting room receives and the direction its windows face when choosing a colour scheme. Pale colours are usually considered the most effective solution to a lack of light and space, but sometimes a better approach to a dark, gloomy room is simply to accept that it is never really going to become a light, bright room. Concentrate instead on making it appear as welcoming as possible with a subtle scheme of soft, warm colours.

Existing possessions such as a picture or beautiful rug might make the perfect starting point for the colour scheme of the room. Sometimes a scheme can be built around one of the larger pieces of furniture such as a sofa. If it is already covered with a patterned fabric that you intend to keep, use some of the colours in that fabric on the walls, curtains, other upholstery and accessories. It is easier to match the wall-covering to the fabric, because, if it is patterned, it will almost always include one colour that will be ideal for the walls.

A faded Oriental rug gives definition to the seating area in front of the fireplace, and the parquet flooring which is visible around the edge of the room has been polished to a high sheen. The tall ceiling appears lower than it actually is with the addition of painted borders.

Plain shades mixed with pattern will increase the sense of space while the repeat of the pattern in one or two places will give the room a harmonious feel. If pattern is only used in one area, the room will not feel balanced and tranquil, but this pattern does not have to be in the form of strong colours and designs. A great deal can be achieved by playing with textured materials that give a feeling of movement in the same way as pattern does.

Texture plays an important part in any decorative colour scheme. Smooth surfaces reflect light and make colours seem brighter and, if shiny as well, may be altered by other colours they take up. Conversely, rough surfaces make colours appear darker; hence, a tweedy-textured fabric may appear darker than the self-same colour in silk. It is also important to co-ordinate samples for a scheme under the type of lighting in which they will eventually be seen, as different types of light can radically change colours.

The best twentieth century designers have produced subtle, well-balanced colour schemes that have fitted the distinctive relaxed mood of the country house particularly well. Sweet, pretty colours are balanced with 'muddy' ones. Just as a meal that consisted entirely of sweet foods would be indigestible without savoury foods, so a successful colour scheme needs contrast.

In order to achieve this, colours are sometimes 'smoked' with a little black or deliberately 'faded'. Tea-dyeing fabrics is one popular method, but bleaching strong-coloured fabrics so that there is just a hint of the original colour left also produces marvellous results.

The contrast of the cool white walls and upholstery against the dark woods gives this sitting room an almost colonial atmosphere. Brass and silver ornaments provide an interesting contrast of texture and finish.

White has become a fashionable colour for interiors and for sitting rooms in particular. It looks wonderful against dark wood, as demonstrated by the photograph on the left. To soften the contrast, you could add another colour, such as pink, to it.

Conversely, warm colours should have a slightly faded look and blacks, if used, should be slightly bleached. A black that appears to have been faded over the years to an almost grey shade is not only a practical finish for a skirting (baseboard) but also gives good definition to the room and a frame for the floorcovering.

Doors take on more depth and character if painted in two or three shades of white or beige, using the darkest for shadowy areas on the panels and the lightest for highlights.

Tapestries lend themselves to large expanses of wall and tall ceilings. Dark green walls make a surprisingly effective background for the subtle beiges, blues and soft reds of this tapestry. The high-backed damask-covered chair picks up the red in the tapestry, and the shape of the ornate frame around the coat of arms above the fireplace is reflected in the central design of the tapestry.

Where the room has good views, light clear colours will complement these and appear to extend the room itself rather than vying for attention with it. The fresh pastel colours mixed with white, so reminiscent of the schemes of Robert Adam (see page 22), would be a perfect solution. Lavender is a colour that Adam used a great deal and would not be too cloying if used in small quantities with a sophisticated mix such as cream and black.

The richer, darker colours popular in the early part of the eighteenth century also provide a good source of inspiration. Dramatic effects could be achieved by mixing vibrant greens with wine reds and Chinese yellows.

Nature can also provide appropriately countrified colour schemes with the earthy colours of autumn or fresh tints of spring. Yellow, whether bright or pale and creamy, is particularly associated with this season and gives a feeling of well-being.

Even a dash of yellow added to white emulsion will give a warm creamy shade that lifts the chill from a room, but the palette could be extended right through sharp citrus lemon to deep gold or yellow ochre. There is a wonderful, almost sulphurous yellow that has been used to great effect in some of the grandest country houses, and it makes a particularly effective background for rich, dark oil paintings and mahogany, walnut and oak furniture.

Yellow can also be mixed with pinks — surprisingly successfully in a country house setting, while green, another colour that introduces the feeling of nature, combines well with them both. It too can vary — from a grey or Wedgwood green through to a rich spinach green. A very versatile colour, green works well with chintzes and other pastel shades as well as contrasting successfully with reds. It has a peaceful feeling that works particularly well in a country home.

The classical urn-shaped base of this table lamp would work well in a formal country house room. The unusual dark-coloured pleated lampshade will tend to direct most of the light directly above and below, as light is not so easily diffused through a dark shade as it is through a lighter one.

SOFT POOLS OF LIGHT

Although lighting techniques and fittings have become infinitely more sophisticated in recent years, the most appropriate form of lighting for country house style sitting rooms is still the table lamp. The soft pools of light that table lamps add to a room are key to the country house look.

It is important that lamps be placed at a good height for reading. A special reading corner could be created with a floor-standing lamp by a comfortable armchair. Avoid having trailing flexes with these portable

lamps — for safety they need to be positioned near a socket and close to the side of the room. If possible, have them wired with gold silk flex, available from specialist suppliers, for an authentic period feel.

A good way of making a room look larger and giving emphasis to the architecture is to place table lamps in the corners of the room. This also avoids too much shadow, which would make the room seem gloomy and formless.

The sort of lamps that look right in country house sitting rooms include neoclassical bases with tole (painted tin) shades in black, dark red or green, pairs of candlestick lamps and Oriental-style bases with pleated shades. Bases should be chosen to enhance the decorative scheme. This might be done by using a dark base to contrast against a light background or perhaps a gilded base to add lustre to a table arrangement.

It is important to get the proportions of the shade and base right, and also the width of the shade, which will affect the amount of light thrown up onto the ceiling above and onto the table below. A pale shade will diffuse the light more than a dark one. A smooth white or silver lining will reflect more light outwards, while a soft pink or gold varnished lining will give a warm, inviting quality of light.

If a limited beam is required, a narrow cylindrical shade would be a good choice while a wide-based shade would produce a broader beam below. To light a group of ornaments on a table effectively there are shades available that are completely closed at the top in order to direct all the light downwards on to the display.

The soft light of lamps, wall brackets and firelight gives this country house sitting room a warm glow. The pile of logs, warm colours and informal layout add to the cosy, relaxed feel of this seventeenth century home.

A standard lamp provides good illumination here for anyone sitting and reading or working in the wing chair. In addition, the curtains and valance have been designed to frame the window without reducing incoming light too much.

MIXING TRADITIONAL AND MODERN LIGHTING

It is unlikely that table lamps will be enough – you will almost certainly need a back-up. For a combination of traditional and modern lighting, the general lighting could be provided by downlighters or wallwashers, with table lamps just used to provide task (work) lighting. Alternatively, you could have two separate circuits, one for wallwashers and downlighters and one for table lamps. Both would be designed to give general lighting, with the table lamps intended more for a softer light later in the evening. Downlighters are particularly useful for lighting the centre of the room, which may be a little gloomy if the table lamps are sited mainly around the edge. The downlighters will emphasize the objects in the room, casting pools of light on tables and upholstery. For contrast, you could add some uplighters.

Downlighters do, however, look out of place in a decorative plaster ceiling, which might even be damaged in an attempt to

recess them. Instead, use small and discreet low-voltage fittings, which create a similar effect and can be inserted into an ornate ceiling without damage.

One of the main advantages of wallwashers is that they increase the sense of space if used correctly. They have to be placed at regular intervals a short, set distance from the wall, and so need a suitable length of wall where they can be well positioned without problems of glare.

Wallwashers look particularly effective directed onto a dark wall to highlight a group of pictures or prints. The successful lighting of a large picture can often best be achieved by cross-lighting using two spotlights close to and either side of the picture, so that their outputs cross on the surface. This works particularly well for tapestries, as it can also bring out the texture effectively as the light passes over the surface at an angle. Wallwashers can be used in alcoves too, to light books or displays. The colours and textures of plants and flowers will come to life at night if lit in this way.

Picture lights provide a traditional form of decorative lighting. To light the whole picture, they must be at least two-thirds the width of the picture. However, even the longest curved fittings do not always light all the picture satisfactorily. A very discreet but expensive fitting is a framed projector light, which is a tiny light usually recessed into the ceiling to throw a beam over a painting. As the light source is virtually invisible, there is no glare and the picture will be particularly well lit. It has a sophisticated system of shutters and lenses enabling the light beam to be shaped exactly to the size of the picture.

Reflections can be a problem with glass-covered or heavily varnished oil paintings, though special non-reflective glass will help. Avoid hanging the picture on a wall with a window, and tilt it slightly away from the wall you do hang it on. The heat generated by the accent lighting can sometimes cause damage, so don't position it too close, particularly for very special paintings.

If any quite detailed work, such as needlepoint, takes place in the room, some form of lighting that provides a concentrated beam of light directly on the work will be needed. Ideally it will have a tilting shade to avoid glare. Gentle dramatic interest and contrast can be introduced with the use of small uplighters hidden behind objects or plants. As always, dimmer switches will give maximum flexibility.

TEXTURE AND PATTERN FOR WALLS

Whereas flat emulsion (latex) paint in a strong colour is unlikely to be quite right for a country house style sitting room, the textured effect of a decorative paint finish can look very good. For example, a dragged finish, such as that on the walls of the sitting room shown on page 89, involves applying a semi-transparent glaze of oil-based colour over a base coat of paint, then dragging a brush through it before it dries to create a textured finish. A tinted glaze can also be applied to woodwork and plasterwork, or painted on then partly rubbed off the decorative detailing, leaving just a trace of colour in the hollows. Skilful trompe l'oeil panelling and grisaille (simulating stone carving in shades of grey) can also look good in the right room, as illustrated by the sitting room on page 78.

Wallpaper provides an effective way of introducing colour and pattern into the room, and it can also be used to create mood, atmosphere and period style. There is a vast range of wallpapers to choose from, including authentic 'document' papers based on designs from particular style periods. Wallpapers in a Regency stripe, large

*Trompe l'oeil work
has been used to
great effect in this
sitting room to create
the appearance of
panelling and ornate
plasterwork. A feeling
of depth has been
given to the cornicing
with a narrow strip
of marbling above it.*

damask pattern or textured effects similar to a paint finish are all suitably sophisticated for a country house style sitting room.

Conventional wisdom says that small-scale papers should only be used in small rooms, and large-scale papers in large rooms. However, a large pattern can sometimes be very dramatic in a small room, where it may look more like a motif. Conversely, if a small-scale pattern looks like only a textural effect when viewed from across a large room, this may be exactly the effect that is wanted.

Covering the walls with fabric (see page 154) is a good way of introducing texture, as the photograph on the right demonstrates. It can give a great feeling of tranquillity and, depending on the fabric chosen, a certain feeling of luxury. It also makes a good background for antique furniture and

Rich red damask-covered walls with a delicate gold filet give this sitting room a feeling of great luxury. They make an excellent foil for the gilt-framed paintings and gilded pelmet cornice. The softly gathered curtain valance in gold carries a deep inset border in a fabric similar to that on the walls and, in complete contrast, the cornice around the ceiling is in a pale green with detailing picked out in white.

An elegant example of scarf drapery at Ayr Mount, a Federal period home in North Carolina. The treatment softens the line of the architecture but in no way overwhelms it. The bobble fringe adds a decorative touch.

paintings. The designer David Hicks (see page 35) uses unusual materials such as canvas for this purpose.

Tapestries, such as the one shown on page 73, have a long tradition of decorating the walls of country houses, and in a fairly grand, high-ceilinged room will still look superb. A tapestry can look good in a smaller-scale room too, but if the decor isn't handled carefully, the hanging may dominate.

OPTIONS FOR FLOORS

Fine polished wood floors dotted with rugs are a feature of many country house sitting rooms, such as the one shown on page 71. Older properties often have wood block or parquet flooring, but if you do not, you could investigate buying reclaimed wood flooring from an architectural salvage yard. Or it can be laid from new, either in the traditional herringbone pattern or in more complex designs with inlaid strips or contrasting

woods. New wood strip flooring is also widely available. Wood floors can be laid on a timber subfloor, concrete or a cement screed but will need sealing afterwards.

Old floorboards in a house can often be sanded down and restored to their former glory. Because it was usual to have the best-quality timber for the ground-floor floorboards, sitting room floorboards might well be worth restoring. However, this process does entail an enormous amount of work. If heavy building work is being done anyway, it may be possible to turn the boards over completely, revealing their smooth undersides.

Wooden floors can be stained if desired, and then sealed with transparent polyurethane varnish in a non-slip finish. This doesn't need polishing but it does show scratch marks. Alternatively, sealing with button polish will give a softer finish more appropriate to country house style. Or the floor could be painted with an industrial floor paint (which does not need sealing),

TEXTURED EFFECTS

Natural floorcoverings are very well suited to the smaller, more informal style of country house, though they might seem too rustic in the more formal rooms of a larger, grander home. They make a better base for rugs than most conventional fitted carpets do, as there is a greater textural contrast. A wide and varied range of textures, colours and designs is available, including stencilled and bordered versions.

Jute comes from the fibres of a plant that grows in the subtropics. It is softer but less durable than sisal and is available in herringbone, boucle, an all-over pattern and a bordered version.

Seagrass is made from a strong grass grown in fields that are flooded during the growing cycle. The resulting hard fibre is spun into strands before being woven into a hard-wearing matting. Colours vary from beige to soft green and russet.

Rush matting is made from hand-plaited strips of rushes sewn together. It can withstand light wear but should not be allowed to become very dried out; sprinkling with water will prevent this.

Coir, the fibres of which are taken from the coconut husk, has a coarse weave but an interesting texture and so would suit a fairly informal room. Coir is available in natural colours but can also be dyed or given a striped or tweedy effect. Although it is quite hard-wearing, furniture should be lifted over it rather than pushed.

Sisal is made from the fibres of a dark green spiky bush, native to sub-tropical climates, and is made in different strengths for different areas of the house. Although it is slippery underfoot, it is available in a number of sophisticated effects such as herringbone, twill, boucle and plaid and can even be given a two-tone or striped effect.

Natural floor coverings tend to look better under Oriental carpets than fitted carpets do. They are a very popular floor treatment in country houses.

Italian stringing provides a good solution for these arched windows, allowing the elaborate heading to remain fixed around the top of the arch. The curtains are raised and lowered by diagonally strung cords at the back, rather like a Roman or Austrian blind (shade). A plain roller blind has been fixed behind the curtains to protect fabrics and furniture from damage by sunlight.

or given a decorative paint treatment such as graining (see page 100) and then sealed.

Rugs can liven up a colour scheme, or even pull the whole scheme together. As well as marking out particular areas in a room, such as seating or work areas, they can also be displayed on the wall or flung over tables. (For more about rugs, see page 102.)

A fitted carpet is still a warm and practical choice. One with a small pattern, perhaps with a border, would overcome the potential blandness of a plain carpet over a large expanse and take rugs on top quite well. A textured Brussels weave carpet, in particular, would be an excellent choice for a country house sitting room. Many decorators favour a very neutral shade, sometimes referred to as 'greige' or 'dead mouse', which provides the perfect background for antique floral-patterned rugs.

Natural floorcoverings are often used in country houses and are particularly suitable for the sitting room. They make excellent backgrounds for Persian rugs, as the textures contrast well. They can be fully fitted or supplied as a mat or runner. A latex backing is useful for providing stability in a busy hall. Hair underfelt is a warm and acoustically effective alternative.

ELEGANT WINDOW TREATMENTS

Traditionally, the most lavish curtain treatments have been on the sitting room windows, despite the move these days towards simpler styles. A full and elegant line is important here. Generous proportions, deep hems, full pleats, and interlining as well as lining are all essential for this look. If necessary, choose a less expensive fabric rather than skimping on the amount.

In tall rooms there is scope for elegant pelmets (cornices). These could perhaps be shaped and stiffened along the lines of the

lambrequins so favoured in the nineteenth century (see page 176). Or you might create a graceful valance inspired by those of the late eighteenth century (see pages 42–3 and 80). Swags and tails (cascades) and other forms of drapery need high ceilings to look their best.

In low-ceilinged rooms, simple paired curtains enlivened with an interesting heading such as triple pleats or goblet pleats, perhaps defined with a contrasting edging, are preferable to anything fussier. A simple pelmet, such as the one shown on page 76, can also look good. Alternatively, Italian-strung, or reefed, curtains look simple and elegant. An example appears in the photograph on the left. With these, the heading remains fixed while the curtains draw back like puppet theatre curtains.

Tiebacks not only make the curtains hang more gracefully, but they also maximize incoming light and increase the sense of floor space. Rope-and-tassel tiebacks are the traditional choice here, but plaited or crescent-shaped tiebacks could also be used, or brass holdbacks in a Victorian-style room.

For tall windows, Roman blinds (shades) are an elegant alternative, particularly if you like a clean, unfussy look. If you are lucky enough to have original shutters, you probably will not need to use curtains at all. Simple scarf drapery above a curtainless sash window, or with plain, sheer muslin curtains, was popular during America's Federal period and can still look good today, as the photograph of the Federal period sitting room on page 80 shows.

If you have a good view from your windows, don't obscure it with sheers. If you do not, and if privacy is a consideration, simple under-curtains of lace, linen or thin taffeta will allow the light to filter through. These will also help to protect the main curtains from sunlight.

Textiles and trimmings play an important part in the decoration of this sitting room. Damask and silk have been mixed with corduroy and tapestry in the cushions on the sofa, and a rich-coloured piece of antique chintz has been casually thrown over the arm. Thick, tactile trimmings have been used on the cushions and a deep, delicate fringe on the swags and tails draped over the window.

RICH TEXTILES AND TRIMMINGS

When choosing fabrics for soft furnishings and upholstery, avoid too much co-ordination. An interesting mixture of colours and textures, such as in the sitting room shown on the right, is much more typical of the country house sitting room than a fussy or overdecorated scheme. More often than not, the colours are gentle and undemanding.

Silk has traditionally been used a great deal for curtains in formal rooms. It does look wonderful, but its tendency to fade badly and even rot in sunlight makes it an impractical choice. Lining and interlining curtains will protect the fabric, as will secondary blinds or under-curtains.

The beautiful soft woollen fabrics available today are ideal for the simpler country house sitting rooms, as are textured weaves. Richly coloured plain fabrics could be suitable for a sitting room in a late eighteenth or early nineteenth century style. Crewel work and linen union – a mixture of linen and cotton fabric – in muted patterns work well in most older houses. In fact, a jumble of subtle patterns is much more typical than carefully matched plain fabrics. That said, bear in mind that it is easier to mix patterns of different scales than those of a similar scale, and it's generally better to have more small-scale patterns than large-scale.

Chintzes are also associated with country house style, although there has been some resistance to them in recent times. Used sparingly, they can work very well indeed. However, although chintz can be used for loose covers, it is not heavy enough for fitted upholstery.

Many furnishing fabrics today are manufactured so as to have the faded look of old textiles. Alternatively, you could resort

to the traditional method of soaking fabric in an infusion of tea. The American designer Nancy Lancaster (see page 34) used to leave expensive new sofas out in the sun and rain, but this method of attaining instant antiquity is not recommended!

For extra colour and texture, make the most of the fabulous trimmings available these days. They can be used to reinforce your colour scheme, add definition to fabric, emphasize the lines of furniture – in fact, add a professional finish to the entire room. Fringing around the skirt of a chair or sofa will also help protect against scuffs. The more delicate trimmings work better on lighter fabrics, while heavier ones, such as bullion fringe, are more suitable for heavy fabrics. Cord and piping are available in a choice of widths, while tassels come in all shapes and sizes, from tiny to colossal.

COMFORTABLE SEATING

Well-worn, slightly saggy armchairs and huge, squashy sofas are traditionally associated with country houses, but smarter-looking pieces will fit in too. If you are buying new seating, or having old pieces reupholstered, choose feather filling if possible, or at least the softest grade of fire-resistant foam. Comfort is of paramount importance here. Loose covers are more suitable for an informal look than fitted upholstery and are also more practical – especially if the obligatory dog will be ensconced on it.

Soft furnishings offer the opportunity to bring real individuality to a scheme, as the chair in the photograph on page 86 shows. Skirts can be pleated or flounced and ruffled, and slipcovers bound or decorated with bows in the same or a contrasting fabric.

Make the seating even more inviting with piles of cushions. Don't co-ordinate the fabrics – instead, seek out antique

Checked fabric makes a charmingly informal cover for a wing chair in a converted barn. The huge Mediterranean-style rustic pots filled with cow parsley make an unusual decorative touch.

tapestries, crewelwork, stamped velvets and other old textiles with worn or damaged areas, then use the good portions to make your cushions. Add interesting trimmings and they will look like family heirlooms. Since cushions use so little material, expensive fabrics that are out of the question for curtains are a possibility too.

Old textiles such as a paisley wool shawl can also be casually thrown over arms or backs of chairs and sofas. They look lovely, adding to the slightly haphazard, unplanned elegance of the room, and at the same time helping to protect vulnerable parts of the upholstery.

FURNITURE: AN ECLECTIC MIX

Country house furniture is an eclectic mix of family heirlooms and newer items, some made by local craftsmen, others collected on travels. To achieve this look, make the most of any family heirlooms you may have, and augment them with antique or junk shop finds that look as though they've been in the family for generations.

English and French furniture can mix happily in a room of this sort, and although the traditional dark wood is certainly an option, lighter tones such as a light

mahogany, rosewood or satinwood will blend in. Touches of distressed giltwood are very typical of the country house look and will enhance the overall effect. Teak and light-coloured woods such as new pine or beech don't look right.

Mellow old pine will not fit into a room furnished with the finer woods like mahogany, but it looks good with oak or on its own in an informal sitting room. Antique painted furniture with its original paintwork (or very cleverly antiqued and distressed modern paintwork) will fit in with most woods.

Because there is so much upholstery in the country house style sitting room, it needs to be balanced by furniture of different heights and scales. Built-in bookshelves or cupboards in an appropriate architectural style are a good way to achieve this, or a tall piece of furniture such as a chest on a stand or a very large painting. It is also possible to install shelves for books or ornaments above a door.

The storage of a music centre and CDs, television, video recorder and perhaps a video collection may well be an important consideration in the sitting room. You may wish to house them all in a freestanding cupboard, or a built-in wall unit or corner unit that will place the television at a good viewing height. If the view is at all restricted then the television could be placed on a sliding section or turntable so that it can be swung out to a comfortable viewing angle.

A less expensive way of hiding the television and video recorder is under a table covered with fabric; curtains on a track below the table top can be drawn back when viewing.

A number of specialist companies now make attractive pieces specially designed to disguise electrical equipment and these can be given special paint finishes so that they blend in with the decorative scheme as a whole.

It's important to have enough occasional tables in the room, but a modern low coffee

CRAQUELURE

The craquelure technique produces an effect similar to the fine cracks and crazing of old lacquered surfaces. It involves giving the surface a coat of slow-drying oil-based varnish and then, when almost dry, a coat of quick-drying water-based varnish. The thicker the base coat is, the wider the cracks will be. If this is then rubbed with a tinted glaze, the cracks will be accentuated. The technique is best suited to small pieces, as it is difficult to control over large areas.

For a similar effect when painting wood, a coat of gum arabic can be applied over emulsion (latex) paint, then when it is dry a darker, contrasting emulsion is painted over the top. The gum arabic causes the second coat to craze, allowing the base coat to show through.

table will not look right (and antique ones do not exist). However, Regency sofa tables, which were originally used in front of sofas for reading or writing, would be a completely authentic approach, particularly for a room decorated in this period-style.

Large footstools and box ottomans, which can be used for extra seating, will double as tables. There are also other possibilities, including an antique or reproduction work table, a black lacquer tea chest or other old chest, and antique tole (painted tin) or papier-mâché trays on faux bamboo legs. A box decorated with découpage (in which paper decoration is cut out, glued to the surface, and then varnished heavily) and perhaps a craquelure finish would also fit in well.

CHOOSING PICTURES AND FRAMES

The wall above the fireplace offers considerable decorative scope. A large mirror will help to make a small room look bigger and to lighten a dark room but a mirror of this sort should never exceed the width of the mantelshelf. Look out for a really stunning mirror, or make one out of architrave moulding.

Choose picture frames to tie in with the overall scheme. In a formal sitting room, gilt frames are very much in keeping. Although carved and moulded frames are traditionally used for oil paintings, they also look effective with watercolours.

In a more informal room, simple gold bands or light-coloured wooden frames might look better. These are well-suited to naive oil and rustic flower paintings and also sporting prints. Frames painted with a decorative finish such as dragging, sponging or tortoiseshell will enhance good prints. Botanical prints have great impact in dark lacquered frames highlighted with gilt. Mounts in neutral or muted colours nicely set off watercolours and drawings.

A variety of pictures are suitable for country house style, including old fashion plates (such as those in the photograph on page 89), sporting prints, political cartoons, botanical drawings, family portraits, traditional oils, watercolours painted by friends and family, and antique samplers.

Pictures always look better grouped than dotted about (see page 65 for tips on grouping pictures). A common mistake when hanging pictures is to place them too high on the wall. A good guideline is to hang them halfway between eye levels when people are seated and when they are standing.

GILDING

Gilding is one of the oldest decorative skills in existence and the methods of application have changed very little since it was used by early civilizations such as the ancient Egyptians and Incas. It can be used to give a metallic finish to all manner of items, from chairs and picture frames to plaster mouldings and lampshades.

The term 'gilding' refers to the application of all metal leaves and powders including gold, silver, platinum, bronze, aluminium and gold-coloured alloys. Silver leaf is heavier and less expensive than gold leaf but tends to tarnish, and so it needs to be varnished after application. Dutch leaf is an alloy of copper and zinc which is available in shades of gold. Like silver leaf, it is cheaper than gold and needs varnishing.

There are two main methods of gilding. Water gilding is highly delicate and can be ruined by damp. It is a difficult technique, and requires a considerable amount of skill. Most period gilding was carried out in this way.

Oil gilding is easier to do and much more adaptable. The glue that is used for this technique is gold size, an oil-based varnish. It is applied evenly over the surface of the item to be gilded. While the gold size is still just tacky, gold leaf is applied, either in the form of transfer leaf (a relatively simple technique) or as loose leaf (which is more complex and requires specialist equipment).

Gilding can also be carried out with metal powders ranging from a rich pale gold to dark bronze, or with gold paint. The latter is particularly useful for adding details to a piece such as a line or small hand-painted design and is applied by brush.

An antiquing glaze can then be applied to prevent the gilded object from looking too new or brash. Concentrating it on the edges, crevices and areas more prone to wear and tear gives the most realistic effect.

Period fashion plates make an unusual collection of pictures. The pink walls pick up the pink that appears in the prints and this is then repeated in the flowers and porcelain that are displayed on the chest below.

It is not always necessary to put a picture right in the centre of a wall – it can work off-centre provided it is visually anchored in some way. This is because pictures need to relate to other objects or furniture in a room. Hanging them above a substantial piece of furniture, such as a fireplace, sofa or chest visually anchors them.

GROUPINGS

Collections and family memorabilia proliferate in the country house sitting room. They can be grouped on display shelves, table tops or the top of a piano (not recommended by musicians!). If placed on a fabric-covered table, use a plain fabric rather than chintz or some other pattern that fights with the objects for attention.

If there is a common link between the items, perhaps in colour or in subject matter, the collection will have more impact. One way of pulling a display together is to place it on a decorative tray. Another idea is literally to link two dissimilar items – a painting and a china plate, for example – by hanging one above the other from a silk picture sash.

ANOTHER DIMENSION

Pots or busts displayed on wall brackets are also appropriate and will add another dimension to the wall decoration. Here, too, they could be linked in theme to the wall decoration.

Antique pieces such as porcelain, toleware (painted tinware) and wine coolers make wonderful containers for flower arrangements. Even if they are cracked and have a tendency to leak, they can always be lined to make them usable.

THE DINING ROOM

DEVELOPMENT OF THE DINING ROOM

Although lavish entertaining took place in the great hall and, after the fourteenth century, in the great chamber, the increased desire for privacy that developed in the late Middle Ages meant that smaller chambers or parlours began to be used for more intimate meals. This was also where the ladies would eat when the feasts were men-only affairs.

Thus, by the beginning of the sixteenth century, important meals were being eaten in the great chamber and informal meals in the parlour. During that century and the next, the great chamber came to be called the great dining chamber or the dining chamber. Furniture for the dining chamber became more varied and the seating more comfortable.

By the eighteenth century a separate dining room had become an essential for all houses of any importance. The larger country houses used it for entertaining company and still often used the parlour as a family eating and sitting room. The dining room itself was at least as large as the other reception rooms, and was furnished in a rather masculine style.

At about this time the place setting as we know it today came into use; until that stage, meals had been shared from the main serving dishes and attacked with a knife and fingers. Special furniture was now designed for the dining room by cabinet-makers such as George Hepplewhite and Thomas Sheraton. Books and journals were published advising on the decoration of dining rooms, some of which is still applicable today.

Furniture was one of the great features of eighteenth century dining rooms. The dining table itself was usually large and, in the grander houses, made in sections so the size could be adjusted when required. The table in the dining room of the Federal country house shown opposite is an example of this.

Most dining rooms would also be equipped with side tables to hold plates of food, napkins, silver, knife boxes and urns. The urns would be metal-lined, one for iced drinking water and the other for hot water for washing the silver in the dining room, because of the great number of courses and the shortage of table silver.

Robert Adam designed special side tables with side cupboards which housed plate warmers and cellarets. The centre section of the table had a brass gallery at the back to support plates, knife boxes and urns. Other dining room furniture included dressers, china cabinets, a dumb waiter (a tiered stand with revolving trays) and canterburys (stands designed to take, in this case, plates and cutlery).

An elegant suite of furniture in the dining room of Ayr Mount in North Carolina, with chairs upholstered in dark blue silk. The eighteenth century was the heyday of fine furniture and many of the best pieces were made for the dining room.

The recently restored dining room at Waddesdon Manor in Buckinghamshire is an example of Rococo revival style and is typical of the formal nineteenth century dining room. At that time, each dish would have been carried to each guest.

During the nineteenth century it became fashionable to serve lunch and dinner *à la Russe*, which meant that instead of dishes being placed on the central table, each dish was carried round in succession to all guests. The old system had involved having a servant for every guest whereas *à la Russe* could be served by one servant to every three or four guests.

In theory, this could have made it possible to have smaller dining rooms but, in fact, little changed – the tradition of having a dining room the same size as the drawing room died hard.

Dinners did, however, become less pretentious. In some late nineteenth century house parties, meals were served at numerous little tables, as in a restaurant, and round tables also became a popular choice for dining.

In the early twentieth century, the heavy mahogany dining room furniture of the nineteenth century was replaced with lighter oak or walnut furniture in Sheraton, Adam, Chippendale or Jacobean style. Leather was often used for upholstery.

These days, a separate dining room is not regarded as absolutely essential. Many people not only eat family meals in the kitchen but also entertain there. The ambience in the kitchen can be cosy, but it lacks the sense of occasion a dining room has. Also, the arrangement is more suited to the neat and tidy cook, as the detritus of cooking pots and dirty plates can look unappealing as the meal proceeds.

Today, this room is often made to fulfil other functions too, being transformed into a dining room when required. Nevertheless, no self-respecting country house would be without one. If you want to create this style throughout your home, it is worth devoting a room to the dining room if at all possible, even if it does have to accommodate other functions as well.

(Right) A highly polished oak refectory table and Windsor chairs combined with a wrought iron chandelier, plain linen Roman blind (shade) and simple flower arrangement give this dining room a puritanical air.

(Far right) In the seventeenth century, seating became more varied and was often softened with cushions covered with Turkeywork, which imitated the very expensive rugs that were imported from Turkey. The table, bench and chairs shown here create a very similar effect.

PLANNING THE DINING ROOM

Think about how you can put this room to the best use. If it cannot be devoted exclusively to dining, perhaps it could double as a library – books make an atmospheric background to dining, and the dining table would be useful as a library table too. Or it could be a billiards room (though it is not advisable to cover the billards table and use it as a dining table – its construction makes it too uncomfortable). With the right storage pieces, a study or family room by day could be quickly transformed into a dining room by night. The time of day when it will be used, as well as the purposes it will actually be put to, will affect the decor and furnishings.

If you do a great deal of entertaining, an extending table, or possibly two dining tables, will allow for large numbers as well as more intimate family meals. Another alternative is to supplement the main dining table by creating an intimate arrangement at one end of the room. This could perhaps feature a banquette (a type of bench, originating in Provence) set in a recess. The recess could be created with built-in cupboards or the seat could be part of a window seat.

If it is possible to have one door for guests to enter and leave from, and another for access to and from the kitchen, this will help prevent bottlenecks.

Traditionally a dining room is a place of ceremony – one of the rooms in the house where the most impact is required. In the dining rooms of grand country houses, the architecture dictates a certain formality, and architectural elements such as arches, cornices and columns are usually emphasized. In smaller country houses, the dining rooms are more relaxed but there is still usually an underlying formality.

THE DINING TABLE AND CHAIRS

The dining table will almost certainly be the focal point of the room, whether it is a beautiful antique or simply made from plywood or MDF (medium density fibreboard) and covered with a cloth. Rectangular tables have a medieval feel, while oval ones seem more eighteenth century. Round tables, which are so good for easy relaxed conversation, have early to mid nineteenth century overtones.

The upholstery of the chairs will to a large extent be dictated by the style of the room and the chairs themselves. Square-backed, heavily carved oak chairs, perhaps leather-covered and close-nailed, are reminiscent of sixteenth and seventeenth century chairs. They would be at home in a heavily beamed dining room or in an early twentieth century medieval or Tudor revival country house.

Chippendale-style chairs with interlaced ribbon backs, Hepplewhite-style chairs with shield and oval backs or delicate Sheraton-style chairs, perhaps rectangular-backed with painted decoration, would fit into a late eighteenth century style dining room. However, they could look just as good in a nineteenth century style decor, since a revival of these styles was popular then. The chairs could be upholstered either to match the curtains or in a pretty contrasting colour. It is currently unfashionable to use applied trimmings on chairs like these, except self-piping which gives a neat but unostentatious finish.

Chairs with classical motifs and sabre legs conjure up an early nineteenth century mood, especially if covered with plain striped or delicately sprigged upholstery fabric.

Furniture and fabrics were so expensive in earlier centuries that the greatest care was taken to preserve them. The main fabric was often protected by slipcovers which looked very attractive in their own right, and this idea adapts very happily for use in country house style dining rooms today.

The decorative possibilities for slip-covers are endless. They can be casual in plains or fresh checks, or more tailored in loose covers. They can be made up in bold and strikingly patterned fabrics, tied with bows, smartly monogrammed or even designed to carry an arrangement of flowers in a pocket at the back of the chair.

Some dining chairs, of course, are not upholstered at all but are designed to take a squab cushion, usually tied to the chair with cords or ribbons. The cushions can be self-piped or given a contrasting trim. For all these things, washable or dry-cleanable fabrics and removable covers are a practical choice in a dining room.

FURNITURE FOR STORAGE

It is very convenient to store all the china, glass, cutlery and table linen in the dining room itself. In earlier times many country houses had a butler's pantry for this purpose, and usually a butler to go with it. Assisted by various underlings, the butler would carry the necessary items into the dining room. These days, when the busy hostess is likely to be arranging every detail of a meal herself, having everything to hand is a great time-saver. If the dining room is also fulfilling other functions, such as being a playroom or study, storage is needed so that clutter can be quickly swept out of sight when the change-over occurs.

This storage could be in freestanding or built-in cupboards. If space allows, a pair of floor-to-ceiling cupboards could create the perfect recess for banquette (bench) seating, and an intimate dining area. A fireplace often provides recesses on either side in which cupboards could be built. These could be turned into a decorative feature with enclosed cupboards at the base to house equipment, and open display shelving above. If the backs of these shelves are painted a warm colour, or lined with a warm-coloured fabric or wallpaper and then well lit, they will become a softly glowing feature at night.

A dresser (hutch) will provide valuable storage space too. Though more associated with the kitchen, it will not look out of place in an informal country house dining room, provided the wood is in keeping with the rest of the room. Mahogany or decoratively painted hanging display shelves are another attractive option.

Freestanding or hanging corner cupboards made of mahogany or pine were used a great deal in the eighteenth and nineteenth centuries and look particularly good in dining rooms. Antique cupboards are still available, but some of the reproductions currently being made look remarkably like genuinely old furniture.

Many sideboards provide storage. Chiffoniers (small cupboards with a top that forms a sideboard) have several interior shelves which are good for storing table linen and mats, silver and glass, though they are not always deep enough for the larger plates or serving dishes. The panels of the cupboard doors often have a grille behind which fabric is placed as a decorative feature.

Old chests and armoires (large freestanding closed cupboards) provide generous and appropriate storage suited to a country house style dining room, and storage cupboards or chests can be specially made to match an existing piece of

to a galleried landing; a good example of this is the hall at Chatsworth, shown on page 49. As the century progressed the hall became smaller and less important, and by 1700 had become simply a large vestibule from which the stairs ascended. It still had a large fireplace with a chimneypiece above and a certain amount of furniture, especially chairs, a table, and a longcase clock. The floor was tiled or stone-flagged with a coloured rug in front of the fire.

The hall developed a new importance as an imposing entrance in the eighteenth century, especially in the grander houses, where the architects had often designed the interior details. However, in more modest country houses such as rectories and farmhouses, the sole purpose of the entrance hall was to provide adequate space to reach the stairs, which were usually at the rear to allow the principal rooms to have the best outlook.

The lighting was still by candles though in larger houses this might be supplemented by chandeliers, candelabra, wall sconces and candlestands of gilded wood and gesso or crystal. These were often accompanied by huge gilded mirrors to give a feeling of greater space and to maximize the candle-light by reflecting it.

A fine example of a nineteenth century revival of the great hall decorated in rich colours and a wonderfully eclectic mix of furniture and decorative objects. Mounted stags' heads were often displayed in these halls. A display of plates on the mantelpiece is typical of the period.

By the end of the eighteenth century the hall had again dwindled in size to become merely an entrance hall, though in some larger houses there was an outer entrance hall leading into the hall. Typical decoration included a plaster ceiling and frieze, low relief decoration in the Adam style, painted oval and circular panels, plaster walls and simple stucco decoration. The windows were sash, with wooden shutters or silk curtains. The hall had a tiled floor, in a black and white design, and polished mahogany doors. Lighting came from brass wall lights and carved and gilt wood chandeliers.

The nineteenth century country house entrance hall was usually square and was sometimes entered via an entrance porch divided from the hall itself by a stained glass and wood partition. Until the end of the century the decoration of the hall was distinctly gloomy. Woodwork was painted in dark brown, black or grained varnished paint. The walls were painted, wallpapered or covered with crimson, green or grey Lincrusta paper of a heavily patterned type, and also varnished. The ceiling and frieze were distempered, painted or papered, and patterned in dull tones.

The hall by the end of the century often resembled a mausoleum, as it was crammed with dark furniture, potted plants and ornaments, and was dimly lit by gas, oil lamps or sometimes candles. Large, solemn pictures obscured most of the remaining wall space, and the floor was tiled or of stone. It was occasionally covered with heavy oilcloth with designs in crude colours.

As part of the Gothic revival, the concept of the 'great hall' enjoyed a revival too during the nineteenth century. Like the example shown opposite, it tended to be a multi-purpose room that was used as a year-round living room, as well as for grander occasions such as balls. Sometimes it would house a billiards table or an organ, and it was frequently used for games, charades and amateur theatricals. It often included a staircase so that the descent of the ladies, after they had changed for dinner, could be admired by the assembled party.

By 1900 the decoration of the entrance hall had simplified a little, with fewer pieces of furniture, prints on the walls to replace large pictures and more adequate artificial lighting. The walls were still usually in a very dark colour, but the ceiling was a light distempered colour and the floor either dark stained oak or polished tiles with Oriental rugs.

In the 1930s, murals and trompe l'oeil work were used a great deal in halls and reception rooms. Often executed by talented artists such as Rex Whistler and Alan Walton, they brought new life to the interiors of country houses. As the twentieth century progressed, country house halls tended to become lighter and brighter and a place of welcome, reflecting the ambience of the house itself.

PLANNING THE HALL

The entrance hall provides an introduction to your home. It makes the first impression, setting the tone for everything beyond and will be all the more welcoming if it is planned and decorated as a room rather than a passage.

Many older country houses were built with spacious, well-proportioned halls which were often used as a form of reception room as well as serving as an arrival and departure point and providing access to the rest of the house. It was often customary in country houses in the Southern states of America to place an elegant sideboard in the hall from where refreshment would be offered at various times of the day. In many English country houses afternoon tea would be laid out in the hall.

Space has been maximized in this hall with the addition of a desk and chair to create a valuable working space. The decoration is simple and restrained, with cream walls and upholstery and with touches of rich colour in the leather top of the desk and the patterned runner on the stone floor.

Using the hall in this way not only makes it a more inviting room but also effectively adds to the usable space in the house. A similar idea would be to add a desk, as in the hall shown in the photograph above, and perhaps some bookshelves, so that it could also operate as a study or library. Even a small hall could be adapted in such a way and would create an ambience very like that in a working country house.

HARD-WEARING FLOORING

The hall also acts as a connecting area to rooms on the same floor, as well as to the staircase. Even when there is a back door to take the worst of the incoming and outgoing traffic, the hall is likely to take a great deal of wear and tear, and so the floorcovering in particular needs to be hard-wearing and practical.

These days, there is a huge range of flooring to choose from. Materials that are indigenous to a particular region always look in keeping and most forms of hard flooring are a practical choice for a hall. In sixteenth, seventeenth and eighteenth century houses local stones such as York, granite, slate and marble were often used. Brick was used too, but it tends to disintegrate with heavy wear and tear so is not really suitable.

Flagstones are often found in period homes and are ideal for halls and entrances. They are available in large oblongs or squares and come in a range of pleasing neutral colours. Slate is another very suitable choice, particularly as it can be given a special non-slip finish. It varies in colour depending on where it is quarried and can be found in greys, greens and blues.

In a well-proportioned hall an effective decorative device is to incorporate a central motif into the floor design. During the seventeenth and eighteenth centuries, increasingly elaborate patterns were introduced, often with inlaid marble work. Portland stone was a popular choice laid in a diamond pattern intersected with small squares of black marble.

Tiled floors were also found in many nineteenth and early twentieth century halls. Made up of encaustic tiles (see page 185) mixed with plain-coloured tiles in different shapes and sizes which were known as 'geometrics', they were laid in intricate geometric patterns. This type of tile is still available today (at a price).

In Victorian and Edwardian halls quarry tiles were laid with interestingly designed border patterns. They are very tough and frostproof, but need sealing as they are porous. Wall to wall carpet would have to be very carefully chosen as it tends to have a fairly urban feel and the colour would be an important consideration for practical reasons.

A mat well is a good idea for any country hall. In a fairly rustic scheme, natural floorcoverings such as coir or sisal (see page 81) will blend in well and are reminiscent of the rushes and rush matting that would originally have been used in the great hall.

Natural floorings can 'move' and be slippery underfoot, however, so should be avoided on stairs or in a household with elderly people. The hall flooring does not, of course, have to match the stairs and landing, though an unbroken finish can increase the sense of space. It is important, however, to keep some link in colour or design not only with the hall floor and the staircase, but with rooms opening off the hall which might be seen when the doors are open.

WELCOMING COLOUR SCHEMES

Colour has a vital role to play in the hall. Not only can it help to create a warm and welcoming atmosphere and set the mood of the whole house, but it can also be used to correct awkward shapes and increase or reduce the impression of space as required.

The most conventional starting point for a colour scheme is the floorcovering, but almost anything could provide the spark of inspiration, from a painting to a piece of pottery. In a period house or a period-style decor, the colour scheme might be linked to the architectural style of the house, incorporating colours associated with a particular period. For example, the green of the walls in the photograph below was

The strong green used on the walls of Homewood House, Baltimore, is typical of the eighteenth century, when this country house was built. The fresh, white woodwork, and subtle, soft green detailing of the magnificent fanlights, the pilasters and the chair rail enhance the green. The whole treatment is very much in keeping with the architecture.

The plain floorboards and cream walls in this hall will not conflict with the decoration of any of the rooms it leads to. The stencils of fruit trees in Oriental ceramic pots on either side of the front door provide the main decorative element.

typical of the eighteenth century, when this house was built. In an old house it is sometimes possible to scrape back the paint with a coin to try to find an original colour under the layers.

Many very well-researched ranges of historical paint colours are now available, enabling you to choose colours that would actually have been used during the particular period you have chosen for your decor.

When choosing your colour scheme, be sure to take into account the schemes of adjacent rooms. The hall provides a link between rooms not only physically but also visually. It is at the centre of your decorating scheme, helping to pull it all together.

Neutral colour schemes are a safe choice as these will not fight with the colour schemes in adjacent rooms and will give a general

The pine panelling in this hall has been painted in a subtle aqua-blue which enhances the gilt frames of the paintings, an effect reminiscent of early eighteenth century paint effects. The colour works well with the stone floor and antique upholstery.

A soft, warm and welcoming colour scheme in this hall, with apricot walls, terracotta tiles and an Oriental rug softly patterned in rust, blue and gold.

feeling of cohesion. They also provide the perfect background against which to display striking furniture, pictures and decorative objects – or even stencilled motifs, as in the photograph on page 54 – in order to create an impact as you enter the house.

Neutral schemes, however, can be just plain dull if not enhanced by the use of different shades, textural contrasts and accents. Also bear in mind that light colours will show up fingerprints and marks, particularly on the lower parts of the walls.

A strong colour scheme can be very dramatic but could limit your options in adjoining rooms. Nevertheless, in a large hall with dominant architectural features, where substantial paintings or sculptures might be displayed, a strong colour such as a deep yellow, various shades of terracotta or even a rich blue could look magnificent.

Vivid colour like this looks particularly effective where plaster or stucco work is picked out in white in complete contrast. This was a technique frequently used by Robert Adam in the eighteenth century.

In the early eighteenth century, plastered or pine-panelled walls were mainly painted in muted tones such as white, stone,

drab or olive, with the mouldings picked out in gilt. The use of soft, muted tones with gilt could make a sophisticated and appropriate scheme for a hall today, as illustrated by the hall on pages 54–5. It will still leave maximum scope for the colour schemes in reception rooms beyond.

Vertical patterns on wallpapers or other materials will give an impression of more height. Flooring with a well-defined linear pattern will make a room look wider if the direction of the pattern is used across the narrowest part of the room, and fitted carpet also increases the impression of floor space. If the skirting is painted to match the floor, this again will make the hall look larger. Tiles laid from corner to corner have a similar effect by drawing the eye to the pattern.

The use of strong colour on the lower part of the walls, though reducing the apparent height of a room, will, at the same time, make a narrow hall look wider. Another way of achieving this is the use of horizontal line effects either in pattern or materials. Avoid juxtaposing a strong, dark ceiling colour with light coloured walls, which would make the room seem lower and narrower.

Think about the direction the windows face and the amount of natural light entering the hall, before making a final colour selection. A north- or west-facing hall, dependent on natural light during the day, will benefit from a warm colour palette such as soft pink or apricot. By contrast, a south-facing room could look wonderful decorated in cooler colours such as pale blue or green, while an east-facing room would glow in the morning light if the walls were in yellow or ochre. Also, a scheme based on cool, pale colours will increase the sense of space and so would be useful in a small entrance hall. A hall that seems cold can be pulled together by the emphatic use of one warm colour, perhaps taken from a painting that is hanging in the room and then reproduced in rich curtains, some upholstery and an elegantly faded rug on the floor.

PRACTICAL WALLCOVERINGS

For maximum impact, a decorative paint effect in the hall is a good choice. Woodgraining and faux stonework (see pages 100 and 137) are both particularly suitable. Not only are the materials they imitate found in country houses but the actual paint effects have been used in these houses too for centuries. For a really subtle finish, however, they should ideally be applied by a specialist.

In a very dark hall a broken finish, such as ragging or stippling, introduces more light and tends to make the space look bigger. A paint with a sheen will also help make the most of any light there is, but it will show up unevenness on a surface as well, so if your walls are not in ideal condition, a matt finish would be a better choice.

Apart from all the standard colours, further variations can be produced by the so-called tinting system, where paints are specially mixed by the supplier. A number of specialist companies make up paint to order and many companies offer a historical range of colours. The paint charts show a mouth-watering range of colours.

One of the most popular decorative paint effects for halls in recent years is 'stonewalling', which provides a neutral background with texture and interest. In this Gothic revival interior it rises from the hall up through the staircase walls to the top of the house.

RELIEF WORK

The first high-relief wallcovering, Lincrusta, was introduced in the late nineteenth century. It was followed by Anaglypta, a lighter-weight embossed paper. Both were used on friezes (the areas above picture rails) and dados (wainscoting) and also over the entire wall. The hallway and staircase were the most popular sites for these wallcoverings, which were always painted. A limited range of Lincrusta patterns has recently been re-introduced, while Anaglypta has been in continuous production.

A patterned wallpaper can hide the inevitable marks and scrapes caused by suitcases, brooms, mobile toys and the like. The Victorians favoured heavily textured wallcoverings as they were virtually indestructible and could be produced to imitate timber panelling, stamped leather or plaster relief work.

SUITABLE LIGHTING

Because the hall is often just seen as a link with the other rooms in the house, rather than an entity in its own right, lighting here is often not given sufficient attention. This casual attitude can result in a couple of ill-placed wall lights and an unsuitable central pendant. The lighting needs to be functional as well as decorative and to create a

Atmospheric pools of light from table lamps link this hall with an adjacent sitting room, leading the eye from one room to the other and creating a warm, welcoming glow.

welcoming atmosphere while still having careful regard for safety. Electrical work has to be done very early in a job, so it's important to plan your lighting scheme at the outset. It helps to break it down into the three main types of lighting that are needed in a room.

The first type is general lighting, also known as ambient lighting, which provides a good general illumination. In the hall, general light could be supplied by downlighters recessed into the ceiling, a central pendant or lantern, wall lights or wall-mounted uplighters. Floor-mounted uplighters can give a very strong light but are not really in keeping with country house style.

Second, task lighting, sometimes called work lighting, will be needed if any particular function is carried out in the hall. For example, if the hall doubles as a study then the desk will certainly need some form of task lighting. This is usually provided by lamps.

Third, and equally important, there is decorative lighting, which will add drama and interest to the hall. It could perhaps be in the form of an attractive table lamp on a consul table to create a pool of light. Another idea is to highlight decorative objects using picture lights, or a flower arrangement using directional downlighters. If the space below the stairs is not needed for storage, an interesting piece of furniture could be positioned in the recess, and whatever is displayed on it highlighted. In a long, narrow hall, pools of light from downlighters or wallwashers reduce the feeling of length and make one feel drawn along the space.

MODERN LIGHTING IN THE COUNTRY HOUSE

Modern high-tech lighting can usefully supplement more traditional forms of lighting like chandeliers, wall sconces and table lamps in a country house style home.

Downlighters shine light downwards from the ceiling, where they are usually recessed or semi-recessed into holes. They come in different sizes, with broad, medium or tight beams. Basic ones take reflector bulbs, while more deluxe versions are fitted with silver or gold integral reflectors. The mellow, warm glow of gold makes this type especially well suited to country house style.

Eyeball fittings are downlighters with a rounded base that can be swivelled.

Low-voltage downlighters have a transformer built in or concealed in the ceiling. The bulbs are smaller than conventional types and give out a clean white light.

Wallwashers are a type of downlighter that casts light down the walls of the room. Mounted on the ceiling or a track, they are spaced about a metre (a yard) apart. Wallwashers are useful for emphasizing architectural features, wall textures and picture displays. These too can be mains or low-voltage and can provide a tight beam or light the wall evenly.

Uplighters beam light up towards the ceiling. They come in various forms, including small floor lights, tall standard lamps and wall lights. Small uplighter bulbs can be hidden behind cornicing or in the tops of cupboards.

Stairs obviously need to be well lit for safety, but the lighting can also be placed so as to emphasize any interesting architectural details. Ideally, the top and bottom steps should be lit and the fitting(s) placed so that there is no light shining directly into anyone's eyes. Not only is glare unpleasant and potentially hazardous, but it is also completely out of keeping with the atmosphere of a country house. Wall lights following the line of the stairs will give good general light but need to be at the right height to bounce light off the ceiling above, without giving out any glare.

Stair lighting could be put on a timer which switches it on automatically as the daylight fades, and on dimmer switches so that it can be turned down to a very low setting at bedtime to provide low-level lighting at night. There should be light switches at the top and bottom of the stairs. On landings where there is a change of level, the step could be emphasized with a downlighter.

Simple and elegant pole-hung French-pleated curtains complement this Gothic-style window rather than over-whelming it. They have been made up in a pretty small print with tiebacks and bordered in pink and brown for definition and interest.

The style of the actual light fittings is an important element of the scheme and should be in harmony with the overall effect. For example, Dutch bowl wall brackets would be an appropriate choice for a late seventeenth century style hall, while ornate Rococo-style fittings or elegant neoclassical ones would suit eighteenth century schemes.

DOOR AND WINDOW TREATMENTS

An attractive way of keeping out draughts is the portière, which is a curtain hung directly across the front door or an arch. Often used in country house halls, the portière is frequently designed to open with the door. A functional alternative is a tall, decorative screen.

Window treatments, if required, should fit the general mood of the hall. Paired curtains with crescent or rope tiebacks, hung from a pole as in the photograph on the left or from a simple pelmet, would be in keeping with the style. The aim is to soften the architecture without dominating the area as a whole.

In a dark hall a fabric with some sheen would help to reflect extra light, while a rough-textured fabric could look marvellous contrasting with a smooth, shiny floor. Hall furniture tends to be quite 'hard-edged' so a soft window treatment can be used to offset this.

Curtains that trail on the floor can look very elegant in high-ceilinged rooms and will also help to cut out draughts, but are very vulnerable in an area with so much through traffic.

As with pale walls, light-coloured fabrics, especially unpatterned ones, will attract dirty finger marks, mud splatters and possibly the artistic efforts of small children. A relatively bold pattern is therefore a more practical alternative.

FURNITURE FOR LARGE OR SMALL SPACES

In a large hall, like the one on the left, a circular table placed in the centre of the room makes a good focal point, whether it is an antique drum table holding a splendid flower arrangement, or a chipboard (particleboard) table covered with rich fabric and piled with inviting books. Antique fabric in a tablecloth or cushion, however small the piece, provides an excellent way to suggest the warmth and richness of country house furnishings.

Alternatively, the symmetry of a pair of consul tables adds form to the area. Even if you don't have room for either of these options, at least one table is invaluable in a hall for leaving keys, notes and other paraphernalia.

A chair for someone to sit on while waiting or when removing boots is useful, and a longcase clock is not only decorative and practical but also introduces a valuable element of height into the space (not to mention a reassuring ticking).

An interestingly shaped hall may provide the perfect opportunity to create an attractive display area for ornaments or books. Areas next to pipes that have been boxed in are often ideal for this purpose, and carefully placed lighting can add drama and interest. A hall is not an obvious place for displays of china or books, but either can make an attractive and welcoming feature.

Storage is usually an important consideration. Guests' coats and hats will almost certainly need to be hung in the hall

A circular table covered in a rich black-and-gold fabric with a deep bullion fringe makes a splendid focal point in this hall. Piles of books, casually placed ornaments and an informal arrangement of summer flowers add a relaxed and hospitable touch.

In this hall there has been no attempt to hide away coats, hats, sports gear and shoe-cleaning equipment. Instead, they have been made an integral part of the decorative display.

or adjacent to it. If there is no rear entrance to the house, boots, jackets and sports equipment may also need to be housed. It may be that the recess under the stairs is the only place where these can be stored, especially if the cluttered look of a coatstand does not appeal. Sometimes a simple row of pegs is all that is needed, as in the hall shown above.

As the hall provides the first view the visitor has of the house, and therefore the ideal opportunity to indulge in a little impact and drama, it is the perfect place to try out a mixture of ancient and modern. The designer David Hicks (see page 35) has been one of the great exponents of this style of decoration, successfully combining his own customized furniture designs and modern materials with classical eighteenth century furniture and ornamentation.

One way of achieving this is to combine decorative objects of different periods and styles but of the same material. Another approach is to aim for total contrast — for example, a modern abstract painting mounted above an ornate eighteenth century consul table. An antique chair could be upholstered in a vibrant modern fabric. Primitive art could be juxtaposed with eighteenth century furniture, or bleached driftwood and stones set against an unframed modern picture, or panelling used to frame interesting modern paintings.

Though not so closely associated with country house style as traditional furnishings, this approach is fundamentally consistent with it, since country houses have always been noted for their eclectic, highly personal combinations of furnishings and ornaments.

PICTURE GALLERY

The stairwell is usually the largest expanse of wall space in a house and so offers the perfect spot for a picture gallery, as the photograph on the left demonstrates. The pictures in a group need to relate to one another in some way, whether they are similarly framed or linked by subject matter. However, it's equally important for them not to be too similar, or the grouping will become monotonous.

The arrangement will need careful thought so the pictures don't look as though they have arrived there by accident. The easiest approach is to try out various layouts on the floor before attempting to hang the pictures on the wall.

A gilt-framed group of watercolours makes a pleasing display on the walls of this staircase. The four pictures at the base of the stairs are effectively hung within the wallpaper border.

FITTED UNITS

There is a wide choice of kitchen unit styles and finishes, but simple painted or natural wood are more at home in the country house than glossy laminates. Natural wood units vary hugely in colour, from the warm copper tones of cherry through to the dark glow of oak or painted wood, and can be antiqued to give a feeling of age. For the worktops, a tough natural wood always looks good – maple or beech would be a suitable choice.

Ceramic tiles look attractive but can crack, and dirt can become lodged in the surrounding grout. They need a strong sealant to prevent water from penetrating. They are also noisy, and china or glass tends to break on them if dropped. Granite also has a tendency to crack but the softly mottled surface blends surprisingly well with a traditionally designed kitchen.

Marble worktops not only look beautiful but provide a very practical surface for food preparation and pastry rolling. Marble shelves on a dresser (hutch), on a tabletop or in the larder are very traditional in the country house. However, like granite, marble is expensive and costly to fit.

Another alternative is Corian, which is a flexible man-made material that looks like marble or granite and can be formed into a variety of shapes. Apart from its price, its only drawback is a tendency to scratch or stain, though this has recently been much improved.

Work surface heights can be altered by reducing or enlarging the base plinth. Consider the tasks and the position the cook will be in when carrying out these tasks before finally selecting the height. The depth of the units can be altered too. Either cut the carcass down at the back, or position the base units a little way from the wall to

With imagination and careful planning, fitted units and modern lighting can be adapted to suit country house style extremely well.

A well-used pair of Belfast sinks with plate rack above. These generously sized sinks are ideal for scrubbing out saucepans and casseroles.

produce deeper cupboards and wider worktops. Deep work surfaces allow for cooking and washing appliances to be pulled forward to fit flush with the units, leaving room for wiring, plumbing and ventilation.

The worktop should project at least 19 millimetres (¾ inch) in front of a base unit to protect the cupboard doors and make the worktop easier to clean. For the cook to be able to stand comfortably close to a unit, the skirting board of this should be recessed.

Make a detailed list of the storage you require and then select the drawers, shelving and carousels with this in mind. Make sure that cooking equipment is handy and that crockery, glasses and cutlery are adjacent to the table if that is appropriate.

A plate rack, such as the one in the kitchen shown above, is a useful addition for drying and storage over the sink. A china cupboard immediately above or adjacent to the dishwasher is handy, too, as clean plates can be unloaded straight from the dishwasher into the cupboard.

Expanses of cupboard can be broken up with open shelving on which attractive items can be displayed, to soften what could otherwise be quite an urban style. Open shelving is also useful in a confined space when there isn't room for cupboards, as in the photograph above.

The area on top of the kitchen units easily becomes a dead space. Store large earthenware bowls, preserving pans, old enamel containers, or baskets there – all those large, awkward items you don't use very often but love the look of. A neat ladder on a nearby wall will allow easy access. In fact, a ladder is very useful for reaching top shelves and high cupboards.

Generous worktop space is invaluable, especially if fruit and vegetables are preserved and flowers arranged in the kitchen. Useful additions are a pull-out chopping board and waste chute with lid cut into the worktop. Ensure that there is at least 30 centimetres (12 inches) of space on either side of the hob or cooker for saucepans or dishes from the oven. Counters will be

needed on both sides of the sink, though only one ridged draining surface may be required.

If a kitchen simply requires a little updating but the existing units are basically serviceable, a fresh colour scheme and the addition of new door handles and knobs on the units and any other cupboards can revitalize the whole room. Another alternative is to replace the doors of the units but keep the basic carcasses.

THE UNFITTED KITCHEN

The so-called unfitted kitchen is an approach that not only works well in country house style but could even be said to have derived from it. An unfitted kitchen utilizes freestanding pieces of furniture, such as a dresser (hutch) and floor-to-ceiling cupboards, instead of fitted cupboards and base units. There is usually a central curved island, possibly with a rack over it for hanging pots and pans and utensils.

Worktops are no longer than the distance a person's arms can stretch. They are at different heights within one kitchen, according to the purpose of each piece of furniture. The materials used for the worktops vary too with the function. In fact, the unfitted kitchen includes as much variety as possible.

The result is a kitchen which looks more like a living room, reflecting the wider uses to which kitchens are put these days, and which can actually be more efficient and functional than a fitted kitchen.

The solid pine table makes the ideal focal point for this simple kitchen, providing useful worktop space as well as a place to eat. Green china is displayed in the glass-fronted cabinet above, and the green is repeated in the window blind.

*A pinoleum blind —
made from thin reeds
of pinewood, sewn
together — is an
excellent solution to
the problem of window
treatments near the
kitchen sink. Neat and
unfussy, it will
withstand splashes
(and cooking fumes)
better than curtains,
yet provide optimum
privacy and light
control.*

THE SINK

Deep fireclay sinks, such as the pair shown on page 114, and the one above, are traditional in the country house kitchen. Known as butler's or Belfast sinks, they were originally supported on stands or mounted on brackets, but they also look good on brick piers or as part of kitchen units. Make sure that the draining board or worktop adjacent to it covers the top of each side to prevent cracks that water could get into.

Stainless steel sinks are very durable but have to be dried with a cloth after use to keep them shiny. Some of the plastic-based sinks come in a subtle range of colours that blend well into the country house style kitchen. There are a number of other variations possible, including small modern sinks in stainless steel, vitreous enamel or

custom-made teak which are designed as a support to the dishwasher. These often feature a wooden chopping board which will fit over the sink, making the most of the available space.

It is important that the style of the taps be in keeping with the overall style of the kitchen. Tall kitchen taps allow buckets to be filled easily in the sink.

FUNCTIONAL LIGHTING

Recessed downlighters will give a discreet but good general light, while fluorescent general lighting will provide a high volume of light but cast soft shadows. However, to ensure that the working surfaces are well lit, additional task lighting will be needed. One solution is under-unit lighting. Fluorescent strips could be used for this but will give out quite a lot of heat into the cupboards above which is not always ideal when food is being stored there. Low-voltage recessed lights are fairly cool and give a good light. Though more expensive to buy and install, they last a long time.

Task lighting can also be done with adjustable spots or downlighters. Track lighting means that spotlights can be directed onto the cooker and work surfaces or into cupboards, and additional eyeball down-lighters can then be rotated to direct light exactly where needed.

If there is an eating area in the kitchen, it could be lit with a pendant light, which will create a relaxing pool of light. Make sure that it is low enough to bounce light off the table without being so low that the diners cannot see one another, or people bump their heads on it. A rise-and-fall pendant allows you to adjust the height. Alternatively, a good effect can be achieved through downlighters or adjustable spots.

Most downlighters are recessed (though they can be surface-mounted if preferred) and this can be done in an existing ceiling. However, in a very high-ceilinged kitchen, it might be worth lowering the ceiling to house recessed light fittings.

Try to have the lighting on more than one electrical circuit so that the light can be increased and varied when required. For instance, it is handy to be able to lower the lights on the messy preparation part of the kitchen and then illuminate the table for the actual meal.

When planning the kitchen lighting, remember that the surfaces here are often more reflective than others in the house and so care must be taken to minimize the glare. One way is to place an under-unit fitting at the front of the cabinet so that the light doesn't shine directly onto the working area. Ceiling lights should be placed somewhere above the edge of any horizontal surface so that cabinets, shelves and the cook do not cast shadows onto work surfaces.

The open fire makes a welcoming feature in this kitchen/dining room. The everyday tools in use in the kitchen, such as the saucepans and cookbooks, become decorative elements in their own right.

The yellow walls of this kitchen are hung with blue-and-white plates and a similar effect has been created on the screen with a trompe l'oeil wallpaper. The blue and white theme is carried through to the tea-towels and items on the table.

It's difficult to see where the wallpaper stops and the real china is placed with this original kitchen wallpaper. These days there is a much wider range of wallpapers suitable for kitchen and bathroom use.

EVOCATIVE COLOURS

In the eighteenth and nineteenth centuries, blue was the traditional colour for the kitchen as it was believed to keep flies away. These days the warmer tones of a neutral palette or natural woods are much favoured in country house kitchens. Natural wood units vary hugely in colour, from the warm copper tones of cherry through to the dark glow of oak or painted wood. They can also be distressed to give a feeling of age.

Elegant cream units can be successfully mixed with a variety of other colours and finishes and will give the kitchen a clean and tranquil feel. The so-called Mediterranean style, which can be evoked with natural textures and earthy colours, suits a country house style kitchen.

If the units, woodwork and walls are all painted in the same colour, this will give a spacious and restful feel to the room. Soft matt blues and greens for the units will also lend an air of calmness to a potentially hectic area, especially if teamed with plain neutral

walls. For a more dramatic approach, however, the walls could be painted in a soft terracotta or Pompeiian red (a brownish red) which would look particularly inviting at night.

Be sure to take into account the quality of natural light in the room. Yellow can be good for grey days, and terracotta will warm a north-facing kitchen, whereas cool blues or greens will calm a south- or southwest-facing kitchen.

OPTIONS FOR WALLS

The most straightforward form of wallcovering for a country house style kitchen is emulsion (latex). For a really good finish, you will need to use several coats – many professionals recommend at least five to achieve the right degree of depth and richness. There are also paints that have been specially developed to cope with the condensation and the wear and tear these areas receive.

For a real country house feel, colour-washing gives a warm, lustrous finish using a semi-transparent film of colour diluted with water. An example of an ochre yellow colourwash is shown on page 71. The most translucent of washes is made from pure pigment and water with just a tiny amount of emulsion (latex) to give it some body.

Contrasting textures look particularly attractive in a country kitchen. One way to achieve this is to leave some brickwork exposed (though not around the hob or range, where they would be too hard to clean). Alternatively, tongue-and-groove boards can be fixed to the wall vertically below a chair rail and then painted. If the ceiling is high enough, a decorative border could be placed at cornice level in the same colour to provide a visual link.

Tiles are ideal for splashbacks, which have to be easy to clean and made of water-resistant materials. Indeed, ceramic tiles are

an immensely practical choice for kitchen walls all around the work triangle, as they are so easy to wipe down and keep clean. However, even though they now come in such a variety of designs and styles, there is a danger that they can look too clinical if carried over a large area.

The kitchen offers the perfect place for murals or stencilled effects. A stencilled border or an intermittent stencilled decorative motif on the doors of wooden kitchen units can bring a utilitarian room to life. Melamine surfaces and tiles can also be stencilled but will not withstand much cleaning so this treatment is not practicable in the kitchen.

It is possible to use wallpaper in a kitchen but only vinyl wallcoverings will survive the steam and washing. The designs of these vinyl papers have greatly improved in recent years but there is still a danger that they can look too fussy in an area where a feeling of calm and order should dominate. They can be particularly successful on the walls of the dining or breakfast area of a country house style kitchen. A check, for example, could look pleasingly informal, while a stripe or fresh floral design could make a pleasant background for family meals.

PRACTICAL FLOORING

Although synthetic flooring can convincingly imitate all sorts of hard flooring such as marble, brick, ceramics and wood, original or natural types of flooring tend to look more appropriate in country house style. Synthetics are, however, a practical choice for kitchens as they are quiet, comfortable underfoot and easy to clean.

Some of the more expensive vinyl tiles are remarkably realistic-looking. With the help of computer-aided design, a variety of interesting patterns is possible. If the designs

are based on motifs in keeping with the period of the house, or perhaps designs inspired by nature, they could look very much at home in a country house style kitchen and provide a talking point.

Another option for a kitchen is limestone slabs as they provide a practical and durable finish and can create a feeling of space. Quarry tiles are also very natural-looking and come in a variety of colours which include terracotta, black, blue and a 'heather' mixture. Their name comes from their square shape – the French word for square is 'carre'. Usually porous, they will benefit from sealing with linseed oil to protect them from undue wear and spillages. In Victorian and Edwardian homes they were often combined with a decorative border in colours of terracotta, black and beige and this idea would make an attractive feature in a country house style kitchen.

Floor tiles are thicker and heavier than wall tiles and generally unglazed to make them non-slip. Natural clay tiles are fired in

wood-stoked stoves. Their light natural colours, which vary from beige to terracotta, lend themselves to a country house look. However, as they are porous and can chip easily, they should be sealed with linseed oil for use in a kitchen.

Another natural product which has become fashionable again is linoleum. In the 1920s and 1930s it was rather thin, and its poor image meant that it was usually reserved for the least important parts of the house. However, it is now available in tile or sheet form and can be found in exciting colours and with inlaid designs. Made from linseed oil, resin from pine trees and wood flour from deciduous trees mixed with chalk, linoleum provides a flexible and hard-wearing floorcovering.

Wooden floors are an excellent option in kitchens, particularly if there is a breakfast/dining area. These floors can be stained or sealed. They can also be painted, ideally with an industrial floor paint. Otherwise, an ordinary oil-based paint can

The quarry tiles harmonize well with the 'Shaker'-style kitchen units in this kitchen housed in a lean-to extension, and the wicker chairs and pinoleum blinds are very much in keeping with this.

Wooden floorboards that are in good condition, whether they are left natural or are stained or painted, look wonderful in the kitchen. However, the boards will need to be sealed if they are to be practical.

be used but it will need sealing with varnish afterwards. Stencilling a central motif, a border or an all-over pattern is not difficult and looks very good.

A painted or stencilled floorcloth is another idea. The design is applied to a well-primed stretched canvas, and then protected with varnish. The resulting canvas can be quite thick. It can be fitted exactly to the room but has the great advantage that it can be taken up and re-used when moving house. An alternative to canvas for areas away from the cooker and sink is a fine boucle sisal. In something like a paisley pattern it could make a very rich-looking floorcovering for a country house style kitchen.

The attractive range of golds, browns and beige in which cork is available and its flexible durable nature make it another good flooring option for this style of decor. Opt for one of the presealed versions, because if left unsealed, it will swell when wet.

FLOORCLOTHS

A floorcloth is not at all difficult to make, and if it is varnished it can be scrubbed with detergent and water whenever it starts looking grubby. First, a large piece of heavy artist's canvas is primed with several coats of matt emulsion (latex) paint, sanding lightly between coats, and the edges turned under and glued. Then the design is lightly drawn onto the primed canvas, and either painted or stencilled, using artist's acrylics or emulsion. Finally, when dry, at least three coats of a water-based varnish are applied to protect it.

KEEPING FABRICS SIMPLE

Roller blinds (shades) are perhaps the most practical and obvious option for the windows of a country house style kitchen. Available in a remarkable range of colours and trims, they can also be dyed, painted, stencilled or stamped and can incorporate an attractively related design such as a bowl of fruit. They are usually laminated for protection and can be made from plain or patterned fabric. A patterned fabric can help break up an expanse of plain units and can also be chosen to link in with the architectural style – for example, you could use a William Morris design for a Victorian kitchen. Wooden Venetian blinds or pinoleum blinds, as shown on page 116, also look smart while being very serviceable.

As a general rule, curtains are not a very serviceable choice for a kitchen. The moisture in the air can cause rot, and the inevitable grease means that they need constant washing. In view of this, unlined cotton curtains with a simple heading are probably the most serviceable choice, perhaps in a check gingham or floral print. Or just omit curtains, and dress the window with a simple swag like the one in the photograph opposite.

For a breakfast/dining area, removable piped covers on squab cushions work well for cane-seated chairs or banquette (bench) seating, as do attractive cotton slipcovers, which can easily be removed for washing.

COUNTRY-STYLE FURNITURE

Perhaps the most evocative piece of furniture in the country house kitchen is the dresser (hutch). Practical and attractive, it could be an old pine one found at auction or in an antique shop or one that has been specially designed to fit the particular kitchen and even built into the space, like

A charmingly simple treatment for the sash window of this kitchen, with a checked swag fixed to two hooks with a batten above them. Grease and steam are the enemy of kitchen curtains but this arrangement could easily be removed for cleaning, and the small checks would not show the dirt too easily.

The white-painted dresser in this kitchen entirely surrounds the window and is crammed with china of all shapes and sizes. The top of the kitchen table has a green-stained surface that echoes the green of the china on display.

the enormous piece on the left. Dressers are excellent for storage and display alike.

The kitchen table is of prime importance. To look right in a country house style setting, a certain sturdiness is required as the kitchen table was traditionally a working piece of furniture. Scrubbed pine tables, or tables with painted legs and natural tops, are in keeping and can always be dressed up with a tablecloth for special occasions.

In the same way, painted or plain wooden chairs with cushions or upholstered drop-in seats seem appropriate. Curiously enough, Louis XVI chairs with curved legs and cane backs blend in well, particularly with a round table. Perhaps the chair that is most associated with the country house kitchen is the Windsor chair and the addition of a set of these would help to give any kitchen a long-established, rural feel.

KITCHEN ACCESSORIES

A display of china or pottery on open shelves is one of the most time-honoured ways of accessorizing a country house kitchen. Suspended racks over an island or peninsular unit can be hung with kitchen utensils, dried herbs or strings of onions and garlic.

Storage can become a decorative feature in the form of pretty jars or baskets. China containers filled with green plants, and suspended bunches of summer flowers drying for winter use are an appealing sight.

Where wall space allows, especially in a breakfast/dining area, pictures make a delightful addition. Framed samplers might have been a Victorian choice but bold prints of fruit, vegetables or flowers in painted frames look in keeping today. Flat baskets also look good hung on the walls, as the photograph opposite demonstrates.

Open shelving is easily accessible and rows of saucepans, jugs, earthenware pots and baskets are a satisfactory and decorative sight.

THE STUDY OR LIBRARY

DEVELOPMENT OF THE STUDY

The earliest form of study was probably the closet, which in medieval homes was usually part of the family lodgings. The closet was eventually to become a large cupboard for the housemaids' sinks and mops, but at this early stage it was essentially a private room used for devotions, study and business.

In the eighteenth century the owner of a country house would often use his dressing room as a study, but by the end of the century he would usually have had a separate study as well where he would receive social and business visitors, allowing the dressing room to be completely private.

The nineteenth century study was decorated in a sombre way. A typical scheme would include oak-panelled walls (or a covering of brown Lincrusta relief paper to imitate panelling) with the ceiling panelled or ribbed in cream plaster. The floor would be stained or polished oak covered with dark red or grey carpet or rugs, while the woodwork was usually dark brown, grained and varnished. The bookcases and furniture would be in oak and the upholstery in dark green leather. A frieze was sometimes included in dark red, green or old gold and the curtains made of a dark brocade or velvet. The furniture was dark and cumbersome in the form of various bureaux or secrétaires (writing desks) in mahogany or walnut. As the twentieth century progressed, the decoration of the study lightened considerably.

DEVELOPMENT OF THE LIBRARY

Books were not common in country houses before the eighteenth century. It is not clear how the few books, probably a maximum of a hundred or so, that a seventeenth century landowner might own would have been stored. Theological books were sometimes kept in or next door to the chapel, but other books were kept in the closet. Collections of pictures had to be put somewhere, and the larger ones were usually hung in the gallery, with the smaller ones in the cabinet/closet. As collections grew in the early eighteenth century, these locations became inadequate, and separate libraries appeared in the country house.

During the eighteenth century, books ceased to be works of art to be kept in special rooms and were absorbed into the everyday life of the country house. Special extensions were sometimes built to house manuscripts and books. Some libraries doubled up as studies or as a sitting room for the family where they could read and look at illustrations. Throughout the century, the main informal gathering room was the

A special antique reading table makes a decorative and functional addition to this library.

The displays of books in this library cum dining room make a decorative background for dining. The handblocked wallpaper carries a fleur-de-lis motif and the curtains are in a heavy velvet.

library, which was often the most comfortable, relaxed and sympathetic living room in the house. Although it was to become slightly less important during the following century as the emphasis on the importance of culture declined, it still remained a pleasant living room and was often used by the gentlemen of a house party in much the same way as the ladies used the morning room.

By about the late eighteenth century, bookcases were in general use. They were usually made of mahogany and were large, solid and rather architectural in design. Originally, books would have been kept behind cupboard doors because they were so rare and costly, but this system was gradually replaced by open shelving so that the spine bindings could be displayed. The upper section of the shelving was frequently glazed, and in due course brass trellis became a fashionable replacement, particularly for smaller bookcases.

In the early nineteenth century, one innovation was the revolving bookcase, and bureau bookcases were in vogue. Victorian bookcases tended to be massive, and almost all the designs were based on or copied from earlier styles such as Jacobean, Stuart or Early Georgian. Country and farmhouse furniture was frequently made of elm but towards the end of the century oak, yew and walnut also appeared in library furniture. Comprehensively built-in furnishings were favoured. Library shelves and cupboards at the turn of the century were equipped with

solid doors, fine hinges and latches (a feature of the period) and adjustable shelving that was often protected by glazed doors.

Twentieth century libraries became very elaborate, with arrays of shelves above cupboards topped by a cornice which was often continuous with the wall joinery. The best pieces were in mahogany or oak and the more modest ones in pine. Shelved alcoves might incorporate a built-in bureau or flap-down writing shelf. The introduction of laminated wood made it possible to create complex units of floor-to-ceiling shelves that projected from the walls.

The influence of Modernism was seen even in the traditional country house in a more uncluttered look which had its roots in the neoclassical ideal of a completely coordinated room.

For libraries these days there is a great choice of materials and designs for the shelving. Bookcases are often given an architectural form, which may be related to the design of the house. Classical details are also much favoured. The wood is usually either painted in a flat colour or given some form of faux finish.

In the latter part of the century, the major advances in technology have allowed more and more people to work at home, so the home office has become a major feature of the modern home. As space is often limited and computers and faxes do not always sit happily in the country house style environment, the home office is an area which requires particularly careful planning and furnishing.

PLANNING THE STUDY OR LIBRARY

As libraries, and to a lesser extent studies, are often multi-purpose rooms, the starting point is to establish exactly what functions are to take place in the room. Sometimes the

library and study will be combined, or a library will double as a sitting room or a study will also be used as a guest room. A library with a central table can also very easily convert into a dining room (see page 94), as in the photograph opposite.

A fireplace provides a good focal point, so in a library sitting room the main sitting area might be arranged around this, with a secondary area sited against the opposite wall. A club fender around the hearth will provide extra seating without taking up any space. The room could also include an area for playing games and cards.

In a small study cum guest room, the desk or a table could be sited under the window, as in the photograph above. It is not always ideal to place a desk in front of a window because of the glare of the sunlight, but with a desk that is only used occasionally it would be acceptable, as glare is unlikely to become a problem over short periods.

The bed – either a sofabed or a single bed dressed as a sofa during the daytime – could be placed against the wall at one side. Where there is enough space, it's a good idea to leave an uncluttered central area for circulation,

An occasional table tucked into a window recess for use as a small desk for writing letters and lists.

and plenty of space around any wall shelving for easy access.

The positioning of a desk is a very personal thing but it makes sense to take maximum advantage of the natural light in the room. Many people feel uncomfortable working with their back to the door. If, however, a desk is to be sited facing the entrance, this will almost certainly have implications in terms of access to electrical sockets and trailing wires from lamps and computers.

One of the hardest things to achieve in traditional country house style is to integrate the necessary modern equipment and clutter in a way that is in keeping with the style, or so that it at least blends in pleasantly. Yet a working area such as a study does not have to look like a commercial office, since good detailed planning will ensure that the area functions efficiently.

Essential elements include sufficient and easily accessible storage for regularly used items, good lighting, a desk at the right height and a chair that is not only adjustable for height but also gives good back support. Combined with easy circulation and an attractive working environment, these aspects will help to ensure that the study is a pleasure to use.

Similarly, a library should above all be comfortable and welcoming, but again, attention to detail will make all the difference. Effective lighting, supportive chairs and conveniently placed tables on which to put down a book or drink will all contribute to the essence of traditional country house style that combines comfort with a down-to-earth practicality.

The bookshelves and library steps here have been painted a warm terracotta colour and the books are protected by wire mesh. An assortment of framed prints have been randomly propped against the bookcase.

This attractive built-in cupboard houses books protected behind wire panels and files, and stationery can be stored in the cupboards below. Painted in cream with the mouldings picked out in soft white, it makes the perfect background for the richly coloured book bindings.

STORAGE IDEAS

Storage is obviously a key issue in a country house study or office. Files and records need to be discreetly housed, and fortunately a number of manufacturers now make filing cabinets in yew and mahogany to match pedestal desks. There are even specially designed tapestry-covered stools and box tables that look as though they have books piled on them, which are intended for hanging files inside.

Another possible storage area is a built-in window seat with a lift-up lid – this too could house files. Or use a two-drawer filing cabinet but hide it under a circle of MDF (medium density fibreboard) with a handsome cloth draped over it. However, there is no reason why contemporary filing cabinets (along with a contemporary desk, perhaps) should not look at home in a traditional setting.

It is perfectly possible to create a successful working environment that does not resemble an office. Built-in furniture can play a vital part here. Units could be built-in with architectural detailing in sympathy with the period of the house.

For example, you could perhaps top neoclassical-style units with pediments, to go in a late eighteenth century house. Or you might add pilasters finished with brass at the base and at the capitals, and finish the front of the bookshelves with a scalloped leather trim, to resemble an early nineteenth century bookcase.

The units could be painted in dark, dramatic colours such as a deep green or

A standard lamp with a pleated shade provides good reading light for anyone seated in the wing chair and the desk is lit with a traditional brass column based lamp also with a pleated shade.

terracotta, as in the photograph on pages 130–1. Or they could be given a soft blue grey, beige or ivory paint finish such as dragging, with a little deeper colour rubbed into panels or fluting for emphasis. It can be very effective to paint the interior of the bookcase in a contrasting colour to the exterior uprights.

The bookshelves can be built onto the face of existing walls or made to appear recessed by being set into a false wall in front of the original wall. Alcoves on either side of a fireplace cry out for bookshelves. Where space is limited, shelves can even be fixed over the doorway itself.

THE RIGHT DESK AND CHAIR

The exact nature of the desk you select will depend on the type of equipment to be housed and the type and amount of work to be done. If it has to house a few books, papers and pens, or if all that is needed is a corner to do the household accounts or for the children's homework, then a flat-topped desk or perhaps a bureau with a drop-down flap would probably suffice. A base unit or wall-mounted drop-down shelf could also be adapted for the purpose to form a writing surface.

If you work at home full-time, your requirements may be more complex and could include the storage of a computer, fax machine, answering machine, tapes, discs, samples as well as directories, reference books and files. Any flexible shelving and storage will need to be strong and well-secured, otherwise a fixed system may be more suitable. The area may also be used for hobbies as well as work, and if the work surface is extended and strengthened it could be used to hold a sewing or knitting machine.

If you spend much time at your desk or computer, the efficiency and comfort of the furniture you use are crucial. There is a great variety of exciting, well-designed and

ergonomically sound office furniture to choose from. It will hide clutter and wiring, and place the computer screen and keyboard at the right height and distance from the user. Some types are fitted with pull-out shelves, enabling the computer equipment to be hidden away behind closed doors when not in use, while other types allow it to remain in full view.

Styles can, of course, be mixed. For example, a modern black ash desk can look superb with a nineteenth century swivel chair. Conversely, a traditional desk or writing table could be paired with a well-designed modern chair. Since not all antique chairs will provide adequate back support, this could be a practical solution.

In a library, a mixture of different and interestingly shaped upholstered chairs is comfortable and inviting. Stools and library steps, such as those on page 130, are useful extra additions and it is even possible to have a set of library steps that converts into an elegant Georgian-style chair.

Apart from a good desk chair, at least one other chair would probably be required in close proximity to the desk. If there is a fireplace and the room is large enough, a pair of reading chairs or a wing chair might be a good addition. Stools provide useful additional seating or places to put coffee trays, magazines and newspapers. A canterbury (a plate-and-cutlery stand or a small music stand) is an attractive and functional piece for a study or office.

LIGHTING TO WORK BY

A study or home office is primarily a work place, so task lighting for reading and writing is of fundamental importance. This can be done in two ways. Either the whole area can be brightly lit with halogen uplighters or an array of powerful downlighters (which is not very fitting in a domestic situation), or

Warm colours and rich pattern abound in this welcoming corner of a library. The kelim chair is comfortably sited next to a table with a well-placed reading lamp.

Bracket lights fixed to the actual bookshelves cast a pleasing glow over the books, and the hinged mechanism allows them to be swung out over the wing chair to give a better reading light. The open fire and candlelight add to the atmosphere, while the club fender around the hearth provides useful extra seating.

the general lighting may be kept to a lower level, similar to that in a living room, supplemented by a number of task lights. The latter approach is much more in keeping with country house style.

Even where a task light alone seems sufficient, a low level of general illumination is also necessary to prevent eyestrain over an extended period of time. This is particularly important where a computer is in use. When positioning and choosing the task light, make sure there is no glare or reflections on the VDU screen. For the same reason, general lighting should ideally be indirect – uplighters or wallwashers would both achieve this.

The choice of desk light will often depend on the size of the desk and the amount of surface space available. A traditional table lamp can provide enough light for reading and writing and gives the room a relaxed domestic feel. Adjustable task lights allow far more variation and provide a more directed beam for precise

work. More efficient light still is produced by a new generation of adjustable task lights which use a variety of fluorescent bulbs.

Task lighting for writing should be positioned so as to avoid both glare and shadow. The ideal position is a little to the left of a right-handed writer and the reverse for a left-handed person to ensure that the hand does not cast a shadow on the page. The general lighting should be arranged so that light is cast evenly over the entire working surface.

The same principles also apply to natural light, which is why, if possible, a desk should not be placed under a window where sunlight will stream in on fine days, possibly producing too much glare. The most effective general lighting for work on a bright, clear day would be the indirect light from a north-facing window.

In a home office, halogen uplighters can be ideal provided that the ceiling is over 2.5 metres (8 feet) high, as there will be insufficient light distribution if the ceiling is too low. A solution for a low ceiling would be to install ceiling-mounted halogen wallwashers, which would provide a good spread of indirect light.

Ceiling-mounted fluorescent sources would be effective as most are fitted with anti-glare louvres or diffusers. They are also economic to run.

Alternatively, a suspended system exists which has fluorescent sources pointing directly at the ceiling so lighting is indirect and glare removed. They would not really blend into a traditional country house scheme very well, but might be an option if a home office were sited in an outhouse such as a converted stable block.

In a library, traditional table lamps with urn-shaped or column bases will give a pleasant general light, and an adjustable standard lamp with a brass or pleated silk shade, like the one shown on page 133,

The extension of this sitting room creates an ideal study area. The introduction of the columns adds architectural interest and helps to set the area apart without closing it off. The bookshelves are a handsome feature at the end of the room.

would make a useful reading lamp by an armchair or wing chair. If the centre of the room seems unduly dark because the table lamps are mainly situated around the perimeter of the room, this could be remedied with some form of central chandelier or a group of downlighters.

The bookshelves themselves could be lit in a number of ways, including high-lighting the shelves with a row of wall-washers, directional downlighters or tungsten strip lamps set behind a small pelmet within the shelving. Another option is uplighting them behind the cornice or pediment of the bookcase to throw light onto a decorative plaster ceiling. Or decorative bracket lights could be attached to the bookshelves themselves if the dividers are wide enough.

INSPIRING COLOURS

Where the main function of a room is to provide a working environment, or an area for quiet study or reading, colours should not be so strong or pattern so busy as to distract. A neutral scheme always creates a calm environment but needs some textural contrasts to avoid being dull. This could be done with the use of interesting woods in the furniture and joinery and textured weaves in the upholstery. In a multi- or dual-purpose room where perhaps the study also serves as a guest room, then a more relaxed approach can be taken.

Sometimes a study may not be used so much for long hours of paperwork, but more as a private retreat within the household for the display of personal mementoes and the storage of files and records. Here, too, strong colour could be used, but the very nature of a library or study begs for a mellow, cocoon-like atmosphere with rich woods, leather and textured linen.

A deep green is a popular choice for this, but a more unusual approach might be a sophisticated grey spiked with touches of deep rose or terracotta. Apple green and white would create a very charming fresh feel, particularly in a south-facing room used as a home office. Italianate colours such as a deep yellow or terracotta can be an excellent foil for books. Dark walls set off with contrastingly pale woodwork create a smart and surprisingly restful effect.

WALLS: A WORKING BACKGROUND

Plain paintwork or a soft decorative paint finish makes a good working background. Too much pattern would be distracting, but a broad striped wallpaper, if the room was of a scale to take it, or even a simple plaid could be effective. (If there are bookshelves, however, these linear patterns could conflict with the verticals and horizontals of the books and shelves.)

Fabric-covered walls (see page 154) absorb sound particularly well and give a calm, luxurious feel. A feature of the Biedermeier style in early nineteenth century Germany and Austria was to drape the walls with fabric, often white, which was then caught back at intervals to reveal bookcases or a mirror. This could be the basis for a very striking library today.

Wood panelling can make a very satis-factory background for a study or office, having plenty of textural interest and yet providing a calm environment for work. Or you could use a decorative paint effect, such as faux stonework.

For a more rustic setting, a soft colour-wash over plaster walls would provide a pleasant working environment. Plain white walls would also be very practical, reflecting maximum light into the room. It is also quick and easy to touch up if it gets marked.

FLOORING POSSIBILITIES

The choice of flooring will depend to some extent on the atmosphere and style required. Avoid stone or marble floors, which would feel cold underfoot and would tend to increase noise levels, even with the addition of a rug.

For a simple contemporary look, a natural floorcovering (see page 81) would blend in well, as would floorboards topped with rugs. An Oriental or French tapestry rug would look particularly appropriate on wooden floorboards or a parquet floor in a traditional style country house study, but will not be as quiet as carpet. Brussels weave carpeting could also be considered. With its small overall pattern, it too would form a good background for a decorative rug.

A fitted velvet pile carpet feels luxurious and would help to keep noise down as it absorbs sound to some extent. The only disadvantage is that furniture will leave deep indentation marks in it.

STONEWALLING

Stonewalling, or faux stonework, makes a surprisingly realistic-looking wall treatment. The surface is first painted with ivory eggshell, and the blocks are masked off with very narrow masking tape. Then three oil-based glazes – the first tinted with raw sienna oil paint, the second with raw sienna and grey, and the third with raw sienna, grey and raw umber – are sponged onto the surface in immediate succession and blended together. Finally, the masking tape is removed to reveal the 'grout lines'.

SMART FABRICS AND WINDOW TREATMENTS

Leather upholstery is very well suited to a traditional style of study, and plaid or check fabrics blend well with this. Linens and linen unions are good choices too. Damask would be suitable for a fairly grand style of room and could be tempered with a more casual fabric such as a textured cotton.

The window treatments will depend to a large extent on the shape of the actual windows. The possibilities are endless, but simple paired curtains on a pole, such as those shown in the photgraph below, or paired curtains combined with a shaped stiffened pelmet, look smart.

Where there is enough ceiling height, swags and tails are an elegant solution and look particularly good with a deep bullion (twisted cord) fringe. If they are made up in a slightly offbeat fabric such as a wool check, they will appear less formal and not so similar to curtains that might be found in the sitting room.

Fabric can also be used to cover circular or rectangular tables. A simple throw suggests an element of comfort and informality in the room. Cushions, if used, should be kept plain, with the interest supplied by texture (as in ethnic weaves or tapestry) rather than by fussy trimmings or frills.

Tartan looks good in a study or library, whether as throws, upholstery, curtains or even a wallcovering. If the room is large, don't be afraid to use more than one – they often look best in profusion.

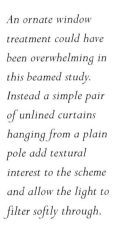

An ornate window treatment could have been overwhelming in this beamed study. Instead a simple pair of unlined curtains hanging from a plain pole add textural interest to the scheme and allow the light to filter softly through.

ORIGINAL ACCESSORIES

In a country house style study, striking accessories can bring the room to life. If table lamps are used, column or urn-style bases look smart. These are even more effective if they have been converted from old pieces such as oil lamps or an early nineteenth century Etruscan-style jar.

The lamps could be used in pairs on a table, perhaps with a low porcelain bowl between them. Or they could be used singly, balanced on the opposite side by a lidded urn with a pile of leatherbound books and photographs in between or a collection of jardinières.

For centuries there has been a tradition of imports from India and the Far East being used in country house decoration, so this type of decorative object would be very much in keeping. Arrangements like this look particularly good when a mirror or gilt-framed painting is placed behind them.

There is always the opportunity to give a slight period emphasis, depending on the wood and style of a table, the type of ornaments used and whether a picture is framed or unframed. An unframed oil painting works well with oak or walnut furniture in a sixteenth or seventeenth century house. A Regency lyre table combined with a gilt-framed oil painting would be a sympathetic choice for an early nineteenth century home.

In a room with high ceilings, a collection of porcelain could be displayed on top of a large armoire (closed cupboard) or bureau. A low drop-front desk might need one or two paintings stacked above it in order to remain visually balanced with the rest of the room. The addition of a bracket to support a porcelain urn or jar is another device to raise the eye.

Wooden boxes are a decorative addition to a study, and unusual pieces such as a clock

barometer or a floor-standing globe can add considerable interest to the scheme. As a study is rather a personal room for its user, displaying personal mementoes, certificates, family photographs or pictures and prints would be entirely appropriate.

A library offers the opportunity to hang pictures in a slightly unusual way, for example on the surface of a large mirror or over mirror glass. They could also be hung on the upright sections or sides of the bookshelves. Some libraries and studies lend themselves to displays of paintings in the eighteenth century artist's studio style, with a variety of paintings in gilt frames covering the walls. In complete contrast, a few well-displayed lithographs or architectural drawings in simple frames would look in keeping with a more pared-down study or home office. Old maps are also very much in character.

Finally, it is worth thinking about the actual display of the books themselves. When displayed *en masse* in the traditional upright way, they may well look rather similar to the local community library. It is worth considering breaking up these expanses with piles of books, ornaments or even little paintings on small decorative easels.

A pair of ornate silver candlesticks frame a diverse group of decorative objects, which include a creamy alabaster bust, a pile of books, a tortoiseshell jardinière containing a miniature 'topiary tree', a silver elephant's head and a mahogany box on which a selection of ancient bones has been arranged. A wooden-based lamp, with a base that looks like part of the still life, casts a soft light over the display.

THE BEDROOM

Until the late Middle Ages, separate bedrooms as we know them today did not exist. Before then, the bed, which was the most important piece of furniture in the household, was in the great hall itself, sometimes curtained off for greater privacy. As the wealthier households moved around from one house to another, their possessions had to be transported too and even the bed would be dismantled.

By the late fifteenth century, bedchambers were built off withdrawing rooms, which were, in turn, off the great hall. These were used not only for sleeping but also for intimate meals, as places for the ladies to eat during the numerous men-only feasts and as recovery rooms for convalescents.

In addition to the principal chamber, the private area for the family would usually include a closet, an inner and an outer chamber and at least one privy. The closet at this stage was a small private room used for private devotions, study or business meetings. Sometimes there was also a parlour, which might double as a guest chamber or be the owner's bed-sitting room. However, this practice had disappeared by the beginning of the sixteenth century and parlours had become eating and reception rooms only.

The bed was lavishly draped with imported silks and velvets. Because these fabrics were extremely expensive, they were kept in special bags suspended from the corners of the canopy during the day, to preserve them from strong sunlight.

Most late fifteenth century homes had at least one four-poster bed and several trestle types. The bedsteads were enormous and costly, with a carved bedhead and end posts supporting a heavy wooden canopy. The hangings and valance were trimmed with fringing or velvet edging in the homes of the well-to-do and with wool in more modest homes.

Towards the end of the sixteenth century, bedrooms again became more public. They were now often used as sitting rooms as well as for sleeping. Bedchambers were often placed on the first floor in the more formal, symmetrically designed houses. Apart from an ornate bed there would be a chest, various cupboards and chairs and possibly one or two stools as well. The bed by this time was splendid, and the bed hangings, curtains and upholstery were *en suite* (matching) and richly trimmed.

Upholstery was rare, but where it was used, the framework and back were wood and the seat would be stuffed with horsehair or wool and covered in Turkey work (hand-knotted wool with patterns imitating Turkish carpets), velvet or brocade. Gold-fringed

In the eighteenth century, beds and their hangings became lighter and simpler. This pretty gilded bed at Leixlip in Ireland is hung with silk damask and trimmed with velvet and tassels.

edges with tassels were usual and also galloon (narrow braid) decoration. Bedlinen varied according to wealth, and included sheets, blankets, bolsters and pillows, and embroidered coverlets.

By the end of the seventeenth century, morning was the time for a levée, when very grand men and women received guests as they rose from their beds or were being dressed. The beds were in an alcove, a fashion taken from the French, and were sometimes balustraded to keep non-intimates at a respectful distance.

People were spending more time in the public rooms by the eighteenth century and less in their own apartments. As a result, the latter became smaller, usually consisting of a bedroom, dressing room and closet. A very grand apartment for the owner or for his visitors might have two dressing rooms which were also used as private sitting rooms; these were often well furnished and bigger than the bedroom. The owner's dressing room could be sited on the ground floor even when his bedroom was on the floor above and functioned rather like a study.

Bedsteads often had architectural features in the form of columns, capitals and suchlike. Floral designs and Oriental patterns were popular for fabrics, and coverlets and quilts were frequently embroidered. Bedhangings were usually of velvet or damask with fringe and tassels and completely enclosed the bed when in use.

Wardrobes were freestanding with cabriole legs. Washstands came into use and were made of wood on a tripod stand designed to take a china bowl on top and

An ornately carved oak bed with panelled ceiling dominates this country house bedroom. For centuries, the bed was usually the most important piece of furniture in the home and was a barometer of the wealth and importance of the owner.

soap and water bottle lower down. By the middle of the eighteenth century it was quite common to have a shaving mirror on a stand and a wigstand placed near the bed.

By the end of the eighteenth century, bedrooms in most larger houses were placed upstairs. The apartment system was declining but dressing rooms were still attached to bedrooms and furnished as sitting rooms. This was often where female guests would spend their mornings. The mistress of the house usually had a boudoir off her bedroom where female guests would gather in the morning. The master of the house invited people into his study. This often had a dressing room and sometimes even a bathroom next door to it but the dressing room was now for its owner's use only.

Sometimes both the husband's and the wife's apartments were grouped together on the ground floor in a separate wing. A common arrangement, however, was for the family bedrooms or the wife's dressing room and boudoir to be on the first floor and the husband's study and dressing room on the ground floor.

The four-poster bed was generally in use. Bed hangings became lighter, and heavy figured velvets and damask were replaced with floral or striped silks. Because bedrooms were now warmer, the curtains were not always designed to pull completely around the bed. Trimmings still consisted of fringing and tassels, but became simpler and less ornate as the century progressed. Bedroom furniture included chests of drawers, tallboys, wigstands, dressing tables, clothes presses, hanging wardrobes and washstands. There would also be a night commode or closed chair.

As the nineteenth century progressed, the new spirit of morality was reflected in the sleeping arrangements. The sexes were carefully segregated in the servants' wing and the children of the family slept and

worked above or next door to their parents. Visiting bachelors were put along one corridor and visiting young ladies along another.

Many houses had a self-contained family wing on one, two or three floors. The nurseries were above the parents' boudoir, study, bedroom and dressing room, with a little private stairway to enable the mother to run from the boudoir to see the children. This was the one vestige of the traditional apartment system to survive.

It was only really at the beginning of the nineteenth century that any attention was paid to the decoration of children's rooms. The furniture was usually recycled from other parts of the house and painted white to unify it. The walls would have been a dark colour and probably glazed to protect them from wear and tear.

Dressing rooms became no more than a room for a husband to dress in and, if necessary, sleep in. Bachelor rooms were usually more spartan than those for married couples or single women.

The massive carved bedposts on this four-poster need no embellishment. The exposed stone wall on the left of the bed gives an interesting textural contrast to the wood of the bed.

A deep flower-swagged border below the cornice adds impact and a professional finish to this country house bedroom

A splendid pair of matching four-poster beds are the main feature of this guest room. The shell-backed chair and shell decoration on the bed cornice give an almost Rococo feel to the decor.

By this time, four-poster beds with a full canopy had been largely abandoned in favour of the half-tester with curtains at the head and on the sides. Some Regency beds were designed as couches with curved wooden ends and sides without curtains. From the middle of the century, brass and iron bedsteads became fashionable with or without a half-tester or coronet canopy.

The emphasis changed again in the early twentieth century as comfort and convenience became the priority. Bedrooms were lighter and airier, often with white paintwork and chintz curtains. Built-in white-painted wardrobes were fashionable and other furniture could include bedside tables, chairs, a small occasional table, a washstand with china set, and a dressing table draped with lace or muslin. Other extras might include bookshelves and a box ottoman. Rugs covered the polished floors. Half-testers were becoming more rare, while the brass or iron bedsteads were increasingly elaborate and often partly painted.

PLANNING THE BEDROOM

Nothing is more welcoming at the end of the day than the plump comfort of a well-equipped country house bedroom. Bedrooms need detailed planning as much as any other room in the house. The starting point for this has to be a list of individual preferences for the bedroom. After all, a bedroom is a private and personal place, a haven from the busier areas downstairs.

The position of the bed should not be confrontational on entering the room. Traditionally, it is placed sideways to the windows but if there is a particularly beautiful view from the room, one option is to place the bed facing this.

Storage will obviously be an important consideration, though there might be sufficient space to provide this in a separate dressing room. A dressing room for each individual must be the ultimate luxury and a room of this nature would offer the perfect opportunity for individuality without

interfering with the general decorative flow of the house. If this is not possible, a well laid-out walk-in cupboard is a very satisfactory alternative.

As with all planning, it is important to maintain a balanced look. The bulk of the bed, especially if it is a tall canopied variety, will need counter-balancing with at least one other tall piece of furniture within the room. A free passage is needed through the room so most of the furniture will have to be placed around the edge.

The bedrooms of country houses are generally quite large, and in attempting to achieve the look, the temptation is to try to fill them with furniture. But there is really no need to do this once all the necessary requirements for furnishing the room have been met.

An open fire epitomizes the country house bedroom, so much so that it might be worth considering re-opening an existing fireplace that has been blocked off. In summer the opening could be covered with a traditional firescreen, or perhaps a low screen covered in a strong colour, then hung with silhouettes or decorated with black and white prints.

THE COUNTRY HOUSE BED

The most dominant feature in the room, the bed in the country house bedroom is invariably splendid. Decorative brass or metal bedsteads look at home in country bedrooms, and bamboo also looks pretty. They are uncomfortable to lean against, however, and so will need plenty of pillows. Another idea is to use a screen flat against the wall on the bedhead. Large fabric-covered foam cushions with piped edges suspended on tapes from a curtain pole fixed to the wall behind the bed make a slightly different style of bedhead which would suit a bedroom in a sixteenth or seventeenth

century style of decor. French-style beds with curved wooden ends, such as the one shown below right, also blend in well.

Placing one of these along the wall is a good solution in a small bedroom. Fabric can be simply draped across a short brass rod, centrally mounted over the bed and projecting out from the wall, and then flowing down over the curved wooden ends of the bed. In eighteenth century France beds were often placed in an alcove, and this is a good way to maximize the space in a small room. Place the bed under the eaves or in a recess created by building cupboards on either side, then add to the cosiness by curtaining the alcove. The photograph shown above right is a good example.

Where there is sufficient space, the four-poster bed, also known as a full tester, is the ultimate country house bed, whether it is in Tudor, Gothic or Shaker style. Although these days the drapery no longer has to keep out draughts – the original purpose – it still has romantic and nostalgic connotations. The most usual way to dress a four-poster bed, as shown in the extremely unconventional four-posters on pages 144–5 – is with a canopy forming the roof of the bed, a valance suspended from the top of the posts and drapes hanging down the length of the posts. These can be used in combination or on their own. Sometimes the posts themselves will be beautifully turned or carved and are a feature in themselves which it would be a pity to disguise, as on the bed shown on page 143.

A four-poster effect can be achieved without a formal frame by fixing curtain poles or battens to the ceiling following the shape of the bed and hanging fabric from these. The bed curtains can be in fresh cotton, linen, muslin, crewelwork, tapestry-effect fabrics or antique textiles. One idea is to collect small pieces of antique textiles and sew them together. The bedposts could

(Opposite) The curtains on this four poster bed are caught two-thirds of the way up the bedposts with rope and tassels in a style perhaps inspired by those of late eighteenth century France.

(Right above) Here the bed has been placed in an alcove and hung with flower-sprigged cotton curtains. In many French country houses, bedrooms were specially designed to include an alcove for the bed. A similar effect can be obtained by boxing in a bed between two cupboards.

(Right below) The apricot flower-patterned fabric on the chair and French bed match the wallpaper in this pretty French bedroom. All the woodwork including the bed itself is painted white, and the bed is hung with a plain cream fabric edged with a cream-coloured fringe.

BEDCOVERS AND BEDLINEN

Sheer fabric such as muslin is inexpensive and gives a fresh feel to a country bedroom. Because the drapery on all these beds is visible from all angles, the lining fabric is just as important as the main fabric. A lining made from a small-patterned fabric that co-ordinates with a larger, bolder pattern for the main fabric can look charming, and sunray pleating inside the canopy gives a stylish finish.

All manner of bedcovers are suitable, particularly an off-white crocheted cotton bedspread or an old quilt (patchwork or otherwise). If you have an old patchwork quilt with too many worn areas for it to be used, it may still look good folded at the foot of the bed.

The simplest bedcover is a throw-over type, which can begin to look rather limp after use, but this can be avoided by quilting or the addition of a thick wadded edge all around the base; separate pillow covers will give this bed a more finished look when it is made up.

A comforter is a cross between a bedspread and a quilt, and can look quite at home in a country house bedspread. A tailored bedspread has piping around the top edge of the bed and kick pleats at the corners.

A gathered or pleated bed valance (dust ruffle) will hide the base of a bed and can tie in with the other bed clothes or hangings. Chintz or toile de Jouy could be used for the valance and/or a headboard, with an unpatterned bedcover.

A duvet, even when it is colour-matched to the scheme, looks too streamlined and modern for the country house style bedroom, while a plain white textured bedcover looks just right.

Luxurious white linen or cotton sheets and pillowcases are traditionally associated

A venerable old bed, snow-white linen, bedtime reading and fresh flowers – the formula for the country house bed-room could hardly be improved.

have velvet wound around them, perhaps in two jewel colours that have been picked out from the tapestry.

A half-tester bed may have a canopy of its own or a canopy can be created by building the canopy out on the ceiling above the bed. Another method is to mount a corona on the wall, or on the ceiling centrally above the bed, to support a lined curtain which is then caught back in swags at the sides of the bed. The curved drapery of the Polonaise-style bed with drapery over it makes an attractive feature when lightweight fabric is draped over the tapebound wire, attached to the ceiling so it extends around the bed.

with the country house bedroom. Linen is expensive and difficult to launder, but Egyptian cotton also feels wonderful and is easier to care for (and cheaper). Other, less expensive forms of cotton feel soft and comfortable too. Colour is generally limited to borders or monograms. As the photograph opposite demonstrates, the appeal of crisp white bedlinen with perhaps the addition of a lace, broderie anglais (eyelet), crocheted or satin-picot ribbon border is hard to beat.

BEDROOM STORAGE

Apart from the bed, storage pieces are the most important furniture in the bedroom. Built-in storage can often provide the best use of space. To stop it from looking too austere, the central wooden panel of the cupboard doors could be replaced with a brass trellis or grid and backed with a fabric to match the overall scheme.

Freestanding wardrobes and chests of drawers offer more flexibility than built-in

Maximum use has been made of this space. The bunkbed fits cosily into a recess, with generous storage drawers provided below.

In this delightful bedroom designed by John Fowler, the sofa is just the right height to sit at the foot of the large canopied bed.

storage. An ottoman or blanket box at the end of the bed can provide useful extra space for items not in constant use. A wonderful bespoke piece could make a real design statement, particularly if it were linked with the architectural style of the house. It is possible to buy or even build-in corner cupboards in which the design is based on the style of a military tent. These look particularly good upholstered in a striped fabric and could be a charming addition to a guest room.

There are a number of styles of cupboard or wardrobe suitable for a country house style bedroom. A wardrobe with a pointed arch motif to the door panels looks right in a Gothic style of decor. Freestanding wardrobes in a baroque or neoclassic style look good and can be adorned with Oriental jars on the top. A pickled wood or light pine, walnut, maple or cherry would be an appropriate choice for a masculine decor, whereas softer finishes and colours would give a more feminine feel. A mahogany finish

can look very rich especially if the cupboard interiors are painted in a strong contrasting colour such as a deep blue. Or a wardrobe can be given a decorative paint finish and perhaps fitted with panels of chicken wire with fabric behind.

There is no reason why the furniture flanking the bed has to be confined to a table, provided the height is right. If storage in the bedroom is limited, a chest of drawers might be a better choice. Another option would be bookshelves with a projecting cupboard beneath.

Chests of drawers are, of course, invaluable. In a spacious bedroom, a tallboy (double chest of drawers) or a linen press is bulky enough to offset the mass of the bed, as well as providing extra storage. The doors of the linen press could be left open to display a colourful collection of folded patchwork quilts.

OTHER BEDROOM FURNITURE

The traditional kidney-shaped dressing table with a fabric skirt and fabric underneath the glass top, is charming and practical. In fact, almost any old table can be converted into a dressing table by covering it with a padded and quilted top and giving it a full gathered skirt. Spotted muslin (dotted Swiss) edged in satin ribbon in a colour to go with the room scheme looks pretty when gathered and is very feminine, as the photograph opposite demonstrates while chintz skirts always look at home in country rooms.

For a simpler look, an antique sofa table with side flaps extended looks elegant and often has two useful drawers underneath. Desks and writing tables also make capacious and practical dressing tables.

Generously sized two-tier bedside tables look right in a country setting and satisfactorily house all the clutter such as books, clocks, glasses, lamps and ornaments that are needed by the bed. In recent years fabric draped over circular tables has been synonymous with the country house look, but today a rectangular bedside table covered with antique linen or lace, or an antique shawl, looks more up-to-date.

A desk such as a drop-front bureau is attractive and useful for quiet letter-writing.

Linen, cotton and even velvet make charming traditional chair covers and cushions, though the cotton might need an extra lining to protect it from wear and tear. Deep armchairs heighten the feeling of comfort and luxury. If there is enough space, a chaise longue is not only elegant to look at but also can be placed at an angle in the room to break up what is often a fairly square shape. If the room has a bay window, the addition of a window seat will make a delightful retreat from which to view the garden or surrounding countryside.

Painted furniture lends itself particularly well to country house style bedrooms. Decorative accessories too will respond well to paint effects; mirror and picture frames, wastepaper bins and boxes can all be transformed. An item can be given a traditional decorative paint finish such as dragging, sponging, graining or liming and then if required a hand-painted or stencilled design can be applied on top of this. This also provides the opportunity to improve the proportions of a piece. For instance, 'thick' legs can appear to be slimmed down with a dark paint, while fresh light colours can lighten the entire scheme.

The chosen finish or design should enhance the piece concerned and not overwhelm it. Ageing, distressing and antiquing are all techniques that make a piece of furniture look as though it has been handed down through the generations. Discreet touches of gilt have the right air of sophistication for a country house bedroom.

ANTIQUING WOOD

To ensure a subtle effect in a country house style home, wood furniture, floorboards, panelling or woodwork can be delicately 'aged' to make them blend into their time-worn surroundings. Techniques vary from attacking an object with steel wool to staining black-and-white prints or fabric with tea.

One widely used method for painted or bare wood involves rubbing an antiquing glaze tinted with burnt umber or burnt sienna paint over the surface. After a little while, remove some of the glaze with an open-weave cloth such as scrim (mutton cloth), leaving the dark colour in the crevices and hollows, where you would naturally get an accumulation of grime over the years.

Another technique, when painting wooden furniture, is to paint a basecoat of one colour, and a topcoat of a different colour, then rub back the top layer with sand-paper or steel wool to reveal the colour underneath. The surface looks as though it is covered with layers of old, worn paint. A similar effect can be achieved by rubbing a wax candle over the surface prior to painting then, when the paint is dry, rubbing over with steel wool.

'Distressing' wood by hitting it vigorously with a hammer, keys or a chain, scrubbing it with a wire brush or making clusters of woodworm holes with the point of a compass adds to the aged look.

RESTFUL COLOURS AND PATTERNS

For bedrooms in constant use, cool, subtle colours will give a more restful ambience, perhaps spiked with warmer accent colours. However, the orientation of the rooms will also affect the choice of colour scheme. While whites, blues and greens will work well in a south- or west-facing room a north- or east-facing room might be better with a warmer tone, like soft terracotta or pink. Striking pink walls, for example, could be balanced with ivory bed hangings, covers and possibly upholstery piped in a matching pink. Alternatively, in a spacious room aquamarine walls could be warmed with bed hangings, covers and upholstery in warm colours such as pink or a faded red.

In a south-facing room, blue and white is one of the prettiest combinations. You could use blue and white chintz throughout, perhaps adding definition with a blue trim or with blue and white bed hangings, white upholstery with pale blue piping, a white dressing table skirt with pale blue trim, blue lamp bases and a white quilted bedcover with blue trim. The linen could be plain white or could again follow the theme with a blue trim. Another fresh combination would be to use a matching green and ivory chintz for the walls and curtains and a bed dressed entirely in white. Equally, white bed hangings can look enchanting in contrast to strong-coloured walls and curtains.

A guest room which is only occupied for short periods of time could sustain a livelier scheme – yellow walls, for example,

A luxurious effect has been created in this bedroom by covering the walls in toile de Jouy fabric to match the bedcover and circular tablecloth on the bedside table. The curtains are in plain cream trimmed with a delicate blue and white fringe.

Warm peach-coloured walls are balanced with fresh blue and white bed hangings and linen on the interior of the four-poster bed while the outer curtains are in richly patterned fabric with a white, beige and rust design against a dark background. The theme is continued with the accessories, which include blue and white ornaments and lamp bases.

Textural contrasts abound in this bedroom, with a wrought iron bed frame, wicker trunk, delicate lace canopy and interestingly limed beamed ceiling.

look very welcoming and the effect can be softened with the addition of chintz curtains and bed hangings. A yellow chintz with sprigs of faded red or pink is an attractive combination. One way of ensuring a calm ambience is to use just two colours for the scheme, which could then be sharpened with white woodwork.

Bedrooms are often thought of as feminine rooms where only feminine colours will work but there is no reason why any pale or gentle scheme would not work. Where a room seems overpoweringly feminine, the introduction of a more masculine pattern such as a plaid or paisley and perhaps richly coloured woodwork, will tone this down.

The use of too much pattern will not, however, create a tranquil haven – though a wallpaper with a small design could be toned down by a plain curtain and bed hangings, or a patterned fabric teamed with plain walls. A pattern in one colour on a plain background can be used to create a tranquil bedroom if the bedcovers, valance and hangings, along with the curtains, dressing table skirt and upholstery, are all in the same fabric.

As the photograph on page 152 proves, this approach works well, for example, with toile de Jouy – the charming cotton fabric depicting pastoral or classical scenes and printed in a single colour on an off-white ground. It is now available in a wonderful range of colours like grey or aubergine as well as the standard soft pinks or blues.

One way of introducing a touch of enchantment into a bedroom is to play with reflective surfaces. Fabrics with a sheen that catch the light, gold or silver fringing and strategically placed gilt framed mirrors (possibly slightly tarnished so that they do not appear too brash) can create a delightful effect.

PERIOD STYLES FOR WALLS AND CEILINGS

The most luxurious way of introducing texture is to cover the walls with fabric. The fabric and a curtain interlining such as bump are stretched over battens nailed to the wall, then the edges are finished with braid or ribbon. Linens with a 'faded pattern' look very effective used in this way.

For an exotic look, the ceiling too could be covered in fabric, or 'tented'. Tenting gives a bedroom an intimate cocoon-like ambience and is also a useful device for correcting the visual proportions of a bedroom that is too high-ceilinged for the floor area. If there are rooms in the storey above, it will serve to muffle sound from there. Tenting requires a lot of fabric, so choose an inexpensive one like muslin.

The decoration of the ceiling of a bedroom is often not considered at all, yet the great expanse of ceiling visible from the bed could be greatly enhanced by an interesting finish or technique such as a painted cloud effect. Simple cloud ceilings are within the abilities of inexperienced painters and can look surprisingly realistic.

Trompe l'oeil panelling for bedrooms in subtle colours is also a possibility. Sprigged wallpapers look suitably countrified in a bedroom, and can be given definition with a plain-coloured border if desired.

Copies of the hand-painted Chinese wallpapers used in eighteenth century country house bedrooms are available today and can lend a period feel. The subject matter of trees and flowers looks as much at home in country house style bedrooms today as it did two centuries ago, and the soft pastel colours work well in the daytime or under night light. The theme could be carried through with Oriental-style lamp bases and lacquer furniture.

WALLPAPER BORDERS

Wallpaper borders are useful to add definition, finish off a wallpaper around the edges of the wall or divide up a large expanse of plain paint or wallpaper. They can be applied below the cornice or coving, above the skirting (baseboard), below and/or above a picture rail, or even to simulate a chair rail or picture rail.

A border can help to adjust the visual proportions of a room. For example, creating a picture rail or cornice with a wide border can make an overly high ceiling – a common feature of country houses – appear lower. A border placed at chair rail height with a darker colour below it breaks up the wall expanse and gives a more intimate feel to the room.

Borders can also be hung to form panels, creating a feeling of balance and formality. These too can be used to alter the apparent proportions of the room. Vertical panels will make a room look taller, while horizontally elongated ones can make it look lower. The designer John Fowler (see page 34) used one floral border vertically around a room at regular intervals, like stripes – another way to make a ceiling seem higher. Although a simple idea, the visual effect was surprisingly dramatic.

Outlining an interesting feature such as a fireplace, window, door or archway, or a piece of furniture will draw attention to it. Awkward angles can be improved with a border outline (though it would be a mistake to draw attention to windows of differing heights). Period style can be introduced with historical designs, while flower and ribbon borders are a charming addition to a country bedroom, perhaps combined with sprigged paper or a paint-effect wallpaper.

Ready-made borders are available in a variety of different widths and lengths. Some come with corner pieces while others may be part of a co-ordinated range. Some have a raised pattern which is intended to look like plaster mouldings. Most borders are pasted onto the wall in the same way as wallpaper, though there are some peel-and-stick versions available.

Instead of buying a ready-made border it is sometimes more effective to create a border by cutting narrow strips from the edge of a wider patterned paper. This works particularly well for making panels.

Other ideas for improvising your own borders are to photocopy an attractive motif, enlarging it if necessary, then paste the repeats onto coloured paper; or to stencil your own border on lining paper cut to the desired depth. Alternatively, you can stencil the border straight onto the wall.

LUXURIOUS FLOORING

Since comfort is the overriding priority in a country house bedroom, pile carpets are a natural choice. Brussels weave (sometimes referred to as looped pile carpet) has an interesting texture that is well-suited to country house style. It comes in a variety of small, attractive, all-over patterns and subtle colours and has an almost tapestry-like quality to it. Brussels weave carpet can be used on its own or with the addition of bright rugs. A rich needlepoint rug, for example, will add depth and weight to the scheme and can also be used to define a particular area.

Velvet pile carpets have a nice luxurious feel which is very welcome in the bedroom.

A small motif in two shades of green prevents the large expanse of carpet from looking dull in this charming and well-balanced scheme , while the walls are papered to chair rail level only. The dado has been picked out in green and the panelling and skirting (baseboard) below painted in cream and bands of very pale green.

STENCILLING AND STAMPING

Stencilled borders can be used at skirting (baseboard), chair rail, picture rail or cornice (crown molding) level, to frame a door or window or create panels. It can, of course, also be used to decorate furniture or entire walls, and looks particularly appropriate if soft and faded.

A wide variety of pre-cut stencil designs are available from specialist stores. Even the simplest designs such as a leaf or fern can be applied in such a way as to build up an attractive and subtle design with a three-dimensional feel.

However, a hand-cut stencil of your own will allow the maximum flexibility and originality. One obvious route is to select a motif from the existing scheme and to use the stencilled pattern to echo it. Inspiration for stencil patterns can be found in a multitude of sources, including original period pattern books, wallpapers, fabrics, rugs and tiles as well as nature.

In fact, natural forms lend themselves particularly well to stencilling as their easy, fluid appearance prevents the slightly stilted look that can be associated with this technique. A design can be given extra depth by the addition of shadow and highlights in a darker or lighter shade of the main

colour. To do this effectively, it is important to check where the light is coming from and where it would fall.

A stencil is usually applied with a special thick stencilling brush and either oil- or water-based paint. However, a sponge will give a more textured effect, particularly a marine sponge. Spray paint can also be used – for the most subtle finish, bounce the spray off a piece of card onto the surface. Or stencil with bronze powders mixed with gold size or emulsion (latex) glaze, to imitate gilding. Soften the look with a dusting of black enamel spray paint so the gold effect is not too bright.

An alternative to stencilling is stamping, which is another very old technique allied closely to printing. Ready-made stamps are available or they can be home-made from simple objects such as a sponge, potato or other root vegetable or a piece of cork. The design is carved out of the surface and then a thick paint such as stencil paint rolled over the stamp before it is applied to the area to be decorated. The pattern can be very simple if done with just one application, or a much more complex pattern can be built up with overprinting and the use of more than one colour.

Simple white muslin curtains are caught back with brass rosettes during the day and can be allowed to fall at night.

Unfortunately, it is impossible to keep all the pile lying in the same direction, however carefully the vacuuming is done.

Natural floorcoverings always looks right in a country house style bedroom. Although coir or sisal will feel somewhat rough underfoot, the relatively new pure wool versions are much softer without losing the attractive textured effect. They come in a range of soft autumnal golds, browns and beiges which blend in well with most colour schemes.

COUNTRY-STYLE WINDOW TREATMENTS

A country house style bedroom is the ideal place for soft, pretty curtains, though fussy details are to be avoided as they will distract from the general air of calm and tranquillity. The window shape will dictate the style to a large extent as will the available space on either side of the windows and above.

In a tight corner where there is limited room for a curtain to be stacked back, a

blind (shade) might be a better option. Where there is little or no space above the window, a pelmet (cornice) would cut out too much light and so is best avoided unless it is attached to the top of the curtain itself. An integral valance, as it is sometimes called, adds interest during the day when the curtains are open and looks very like a real valance when the curtains are closed.

Where the windows are inward-opening and might be obstructed by a valance or pelmet, a curved pelmet board not only is a good solution but also looks decorative. Softly draped dress curtains (curtains that do not close) combined with a Roman blind would look fresh in a soft checked fabric. As the photograph on page 158 illustrates, curtains hung on a wooden or brass pole always look as though they belong in the country, and pretty plains and floral and figurative patterns are especially well-suited to country house bedrooms.

For a really luxurious feel in a bedroom, it is well worth going to the extra expense of interlining as well as ordinary lining. The curtains will hang better and the extra layer will increase the insulation and help cut out draughts.

A RANGE OF LIGHTING

A bedroom requires a considerable range of lighting, from bright clear light for putting on make-up, choosing clothing or reading, to soft lighting for relaxing.

The bedside lights should be the right height for reading, and adjustable if possible. An alternative to table lamps is a hinged bracket lamp fixed to the wall beside the bed at a height and distance to give good light for reading. A pair of these are shown in the photograph above.

The switches for the bedside lights should be comfortably accessible from the bed. It is also helpful to have a versatile

switching system which allows you to turn on all the lights from the door and then switch off not only the reading lights but also the main lights from the bed. The provision of dimmer switches on all circuits will give additional flexibility.

Lights that switch on as a cupboard door is opened make clothes selection much easier. Full-length mirrors on the inside or outside of cupboard doors should be lit so that the light shines on the person viewing themselves in the mirror rather than the actual mirror itself.

Recessed downlighters will give a very good general level of light in a dressing room, perhaps with the addition of a few adjustable ones to give the perfect 45-degree angle above any full-length mirrors. Downlighters (or uplighters) could also be

These wall-mounted bracket lights are placed at a good height for reading and can be moved from side to side to suit the reader.

*Antique handmirrors
and black-and-white
prints displayed* en
masse *make an
unusual and decor-
ative combination in
this dressing room.*

used to highlight special displays or architectural details. For the dressing table, an attractive pair of tall table lamps with candlestick-type bases looks in keeping with the country house style and will cast a fairly even light across the face when making up.

Table lamps will give a cosy, intimate light in the bedroom. The colour of light they give out will be affected by the colour of the bulb and of the shade itself. A very soft, pretty look for a country house bedroom is a pleated silk shade lined in soft pink or peach with softlight bulbs in the same colour.

The broader the base of the shade, the broader the beam of light it will give out, and an opaque shade will project a beam of light below and above. To keep the shade in proportion to its base, it should be roughly the same height as the base. The diameter of the base of the shade should also be about the same as the height of the base.

Porcelain bases with Oriental patterns blend in well, or for a more masculine room you could use either the candlestick or column style of base in antiqued brass or painted wood.

ACCESSORIES FOR THE BEDROOM

Possible accessories for the country house style bedroom include porcelain plates on stands, ceramic jardinières, silver photograph frames displaying family photographs and small enamel boxes. Pictures might include classically framed prints with prettily coloured mounts, small oils in ornate gilt frames, needlework set in verre églomisé (glass decorated with gold leaf) or paintings in gilded or painted oval frames suspended on wide satin picture sashes. Antique lace collars and cuffs look lovely in wooden frames, and old samplers are perfect for this room.

Antique handmirrors and black-and-white prints displayed en masse *make an unusual and decorative combination in this dressing room.*

In a guest room, lace-trimmed linen towels, reading material, writing paper and pens, fresh or bottled water and fresh flowers are hospitable touches that are always appreciated. The addition of delicious biscuits in a tin is a long-standing tradition for country house guest rooms.

CHILDREN'S ROOMS

The key to the design and decoration of children's rooms is to provide a degree of flexibility. Children grow up so quickly that the practical requirements of the room change frequently, so it is important to choose a layout and furniture that can adapt to these changing needs.

Safety is crucial. Sockets and radiators should be fitted with safety covers, and windows with safety catches or even bars if they are low and accessible. Any painted furniture should be decorated with a lead-free, non-toxic paint and corners should be rounded for safety.

An unusual head-board with Gothic arches forms the back-drop for fresh linen monogrammed in gold and a delicately fringed antique lace bedspread. More lace spills over the bedside table, where a collection of silver-topped scent bottles is displayed.

Plugs should always be safety plugs and light bulbs should be well out of reach. Put in plenty of power points at the outset — although only a few will be required at the baby stage, several will be needed later for lights, computer, stereo and possibly a television. Fittings to avoid include over-bright task lights, clip-on spots, low wall-mounted track fittings, powerful uplighters, standard lamps and extension leads. Many children are frightened of the dark and a low-energy nightlight will give out a pleasant and economic glow.

Children need stimulation in their rooms so primary colours could certainly be used here, though some of the prettiest schemes involve a mixture of fresh pastel colours such as yellow, blue and pink. Putting up a chair rail (if there isn't one already) will allow the application of a strong-coloured washable painted surface below the rail and perhaps a wallpaper above. A themed nursery or children's room could have a mural or lively scene created with felt cut-outs mounted on a felt-covered board. A blackboard or blackboard paint below the dado on one wall would help divert artistic effort to a wipeable surface. Many charming wallpaper borders are available for children's rooms featuring nursery rhyme characters, farm animals and other favourite creatures.

A hard-twist pile carpet is suitably resilient, though it can be a little slippery underfoot so would not be ideal in a nursery from that point of view. These rooms need a flooring which is warm enough to be crawled on, tough enough for toys with wheels to run over and still be quiet underfoot. Of course, it must also be easy to clean, so a good choice would be cork,

This children's room with a tiny sprigged wallpaper and curtains, floral border and blue-and-white gingham covered headboard will last from the nursery stage right up to the teenage years.

linoleum, vinyl or even wood. Rubber would certainly meet the practical criteria but has too much of a high-tech connotation for country house style.

A washable rug could be added but not perhaps till the child is older as it could easily cause a toddler to trip. Pure cotton floorcoverings are suitable for older children. These are available in neutral colours enlivened with broad stripes of brighter colours.

A more creative solution would be a design painted directly onto the floorboards – polkadots, stripes or a chevron pattern would all work well. Again, this could be softened with a washable rug. A painted floorcloth could carry a design for a game such as hopscotch or a chequerboard for draughts.

It is tempting to go overboard with all the wonderful fabrics specially designed for nurseries, featuring appealing ducks, bears, clowns and the like. A longer-lasting approach, however, is to make the main curtains and upholstery from an ordinary fabric such as a stripe or check and to keep the nursery fabrics for smaller items such as cushions and duvet covers.

Curtains in children's rooms should be kept simple, ideally finishing just below sill level. Pinch pleats, perhaps with a button detail or a tab heading, would be appropriate. Interest could be added by using a plain fabric for the main curtains and a pattern such as a check for a pelmet and tiebacks. Roman and roller blinds work well in children's rooms. A blackout lining can be added so they are not disturbed by unnecessary light.

A nursery will need a cot (ideally one that converts into a bed when the baby is older), a chest of drawers, a changing area, a comfortable nursing chair, storage for toys, clothes and bedlinen and free space for playing on the floor.

These days, nursery furniture is highly imaginative, ranging from traditional painted cupboards and chests through to amusing combinations of creative or themed shapes for bunk beds, desks, chests and cupboards. Old chests and bookshelves can be revitalized for children's rooms with decorative paint finishes, stencilled designs or découpage. A sturdy pine chest is always useful and can also provide seating if the top is padded with a thick squab cushion. A screen, perhaps covered with cork or fabric, will hide a messy corner.

Young girls love a simply draped canopy over the bed. The bedcover could match one of the fabrics being used in the room, with a turnover in a contrasting colour. This could then be trimmed with ties or bows and a pillowcase made to match.

Space for storage is often a problem in children's rooms, which are sometimes the smaller rooms near the top of the house. Apart from freestanding storage, the obvious places for built-in storage in these rooms are any alcoves or space under the eaves. The cupboard doors could always be changed or repainted at a later date to ring the changes.

Freestanding bookshelves could be used to divide up a shared bedroom or to create a reading corner. Many beds and bunk beds are designed these days to give extra storage in drawers underneath, and a deep window seat will also provide a useful recess below the seat itself which could be turned into drawers or shelves.

Bright, cheerful fabric can be used to make drawstring bags to hang on pegs for storing toys, pyjamas or accessories such as ribbons, hairbands or belts. Wicker baskets lined with fabric make good storage for toys and are better suited to country house style than the ubiquitous bright-coloured plastic boxes.

THE BATHROOM

DEVELOPMENT OF THE BATHROOM

Despite the sophisticated bathing, hygiene and sewage facilities introduced by the Romans, the bathroom found in country houses of six hundred years ago had reverted to a small privy in which a pierced seat was placed over a shaft. There was also a jug of water which would have been carried in from the kitchen and was used for washing.

By the sixteenth and seventeenth centuries the privy had become a 'house of easement' in the courtyard or cellar which could often facilitate two or more people simultaneously. The alternative was a large pail which was emptied out of the upstairs window into the street.

Monasteries had some of the most advanced systems and their dissolution by Henry VIII provided many landowners with a ready-made water supply system. But it was not until the end of the seventeenth century that many country houses acquired a running water supply produced by pumping or gravity.

By the eighteenth century, some homes had installed bathrooms with water-closets and a basin or cistern in which to wash. However, as this was an expensive option when labour to carry water to the bedroom was so cheap, it was not a fashion that caught on very fast. In some instances there was a separate bath house in the garden or even an open-air bath supplied by rainwater tanks. Personal cleanliness was still not a great priority and baths were often only taken on a weekly or even monthly basis, in the elegant plunge baths that had begun to appear in the late eighteenth century.

In the early nineteenth century the shower bath was invented and bathtubs began to replace the earlier plunge baths. Water-closets, having been fitted with valves, became really efficient and were in general use. Water could now be piped and pumped to the upper floors and there was frequently more than one bathroom in the house. By the end of the nineteenth century all new country houses had running water on every floor and plenty of water-closets. However, in many existing houses the usual means of washing was still with hip baths or toilet jugs and basins supplied from brass cans of hot water brought by the housemaids.

By 1910 most older country houses were being adapted to take bathrooms and dressing rooms. Closets provided the perfect solution to this although en suite bathrooms were very rare indeed. Even in the grander country houses there was frequently no more than one bathroom to a floor, and long queues of guests in their dressing gowns clutching their sponge bags in the early morning and before dinner were

An early version of a bath with an integral shower makes a splendid central feature in this Australian country house bathroom. Pink amaryllis in ceramic pots stand out against the simple white walls, tiled floor and plain white shower curtains.

commonplace. Bathroom accessories became fashionable and included bath seats and trays, shaving cabinets and mirrors, scales, towel rails, soap trays and toothbrush holders. Water-closets were becoming increasingly ornate in design, as were copper geysers (water heaters) and wash-basins. The latter were supported on painted iron legs or highly decorated painted iron wall brackets. Showers were usually curtained off.

Around the turn of the century, American architects began to designate specific spaces for bathrooms. From the 1830s inventors in the United States had experimented with gravity-fed water systems which allowed for sanitary flush. These devices were fully perfected in the 1890s, culminating in the self-washing bowl and siphon jet used today.

Bathroom fittings were technically more advanced than in Britain. Some bathrooms were immensely sophisticated, with classical overtones heavily embellished with period detail. Metal handles were elegantly cast, wooden seats painted with flowers or trees and even the bowl of the water-closet sometimes featured a decorative glaze. Some wash-basins were enclosed with wooden cabinets, while others were set into metal stands. Still others featured four porcelain legs or a single porcelain pedestal which could take the form of a fluted column.

Early in the twentieth century the cast iron bath on legs was still favoured, as enclosing the bath in wood panelling was believed to be unhealthy. Hygiene was a priority and bathroom curtains and soft furnishings were also eschewed for harbouring dirt and microbes – windows were fitted with obscured glass instead. Bathroom fittings generally became more streamlined, with fewer dust-traps than they had previously.

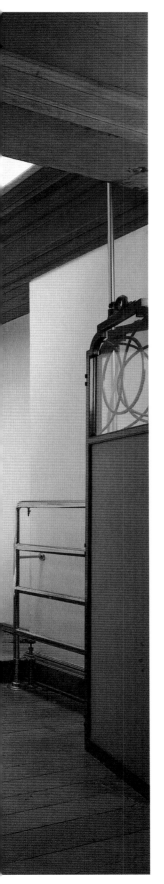

In the 1920s and 1930s, bathroom planning became more highly developed. Many baths were built into a recess and often had a shower attachment. Separate shower cabinets with glass panels were sometimes found in the wealthiest homes. The bathtub on legs gave way to the boxed-in model with a moulded or tiled panel. Bath fixtures now came in clean, modern shapes in chromium, and mixer taps became more common. Pedestal wash-basins were available in a variety of shapes and water-closets were made with a lower cistern.

Today, hygiene and efficiency are taken for granted, but the fittings popular around the turn of the century are enjoying a revival. The result is a bathroom that is a haven of relaxation and comfort.

PLANNING THE BATHROOM

Whatever the size of a bathroom or a cloak-room in a country house, a traditional style tends to look more in keeping than a modern streamlined approach. As with the bedroom, the country house bathroom should exude an ambience of comfort and warmth.

Whereas the modern fitted bathroom sites the fittings around the perimeter of the room, the more generous-sized bathroom often found in country houses allows greater flexibility. The bath may be positioned centrally, and the room furnished with comfortable armchairs. Some may even be dual-purpose rooms. The designer David Hicks (see page 35) famously combined the bathroom and study in one of his country homes.

Sir Edwin Lutyens designed Castle Drogo in Devon down to the last detail. The basin is housed in a beautifully made wooden unit and the bath mounted on a platform. A mirror is placed on an unusual marble-topped bow-fronted chest.

In this impressive bathroom, the bath is placed centrally and glass-fronted storage cupboards have been built into the recesses on either side of the shower. A vanity unit with two basins, and shelves and mirrors above, has been installed along the right-hand wall. A collection of blue-and-white china adds a decorative touch, and a circular table carrying potpourri, bubblebath and candles is placed conveniently adjacent to the bath.

Bathrooms are sometimes quite awkward shapes and sizes but this can often be turned into an advantage. For example, in a long narrow bathroom, the basin(s), bath, bidet and WC could all be placed along one wall and housed in separate mirrored cupboards, perhaps with the addition of a dressing table or armchair so that the room would effectively look like a dressing room. In fact, the most cost-effective bathroom layout is to position all the fittings in one line.

Areas of semi-privacy can be created within the bathroom with short partitions dividing the basins from the bath or shower or a separate section for the WC. A screen could also be used for this.

The first decision is to establish whether you need a second basin, a bidet and a separate shower – and whether you'll have room for them. A common mistake in bathroom planning is to allow just enough room for the fittings and furniture and to forget the amount of space that is required to climb in and out of the bath or shower and to get dry.

TRADITIONAL BATHS

Traditional Victorian and Edwardian fittings are ideal for a country house style bathroom or cloakroom. Reproduction versions are so widely available now that you are spoiled for choice.

The bath itself is the most important decision for the bathroom. Traditional types are made from cast iron finished with vitreous enamel. They are expensive but durable and their considerable weight may mean that the floor has to be reinforced for safety. Acrylic and glass-reinforced polyester baths are cheaper and warmer and are available in a variety of colours, but do not really look right in a country house bathroom. A recently developed type of bath is made from composite synthetic materials which are thicker and more rigid than acrylic, retain heat well and are very durable.

An architectural salvage yard may be able to offer a lovely old bathtub in an interesting material such as copper, which could be the central feature of the bathroom. The designer Nancy Lancaster (see page 34) once set one of these inside an eighteenth century chaise longue with a cane top which was lifted to get into the tub and then pulled down to completely cover the user. Salvage yards also sell old rolltop tubs. Professional resurfacing will extend the life of an original bath that is stained or worn, but the surface of a new, reproduction bath will last longer.

Freestanding rolltop baths with ball-and-claw feet are perfect for a country house style bathroom. Bear in mind, however, that not only will the plumbing be visible (unless you bury it in the wall), but also these baths allow water to drip from the bath–shower mixer, if fitted, down the side onto the floor after use. In a bathroom with carpet on the floor, this could be a potential problem. The photographs on pages 167 and 169 are examples of the visible plumbing that is often necessary with these baths.

To make a modern bath more in character with country house style, you could consider replacing the side and end panels with ready-made (or custom-built) mahogany panels or old-pine panelling. Alternatively, build a wooden framework around the bath and either tile or marble it (see page 169), like the marbled bath shown in the photograph on the right. If the taps are modern in style, replace them with traditional taps, which are now widely available. Where a bath is to be built-in, it is worth allowing for a wide area around it so that there is generous space to display attractive bottles of bath oils, creams and shampoos.

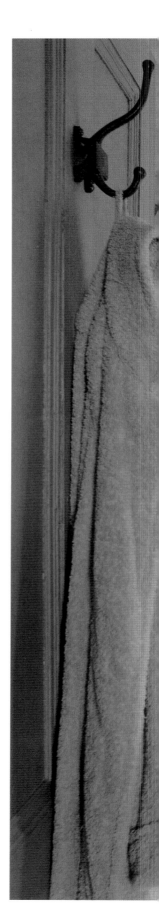

MARBLING

Marble has been a feature of many country house bathrooms, but using decorative paint techniques it is possible to introduce the look of marble at a fraction of the cost of the real thing. The outside of a rolltop bath or bath panelling is an obvious candidate, or the skirting (baseboard) or panelling, or perhaps just a mirror frame, could be marbled instead.

The marbling can be a copy of a specific type of marble, such as Egyptian green, Carrara or Siena marble, or it can be 'fantasy' marbling, sometimes known as marbleizing, which gives an impression of marble without imitating any particular one.

A paint-effects artist can create some very realistic-looking finishes. The techniques vary according to the type of marble, but involve applying coloured oil glazes onto a coloured eggshell paint ground. The veining is created using sponges, specialist brushes and feathers.

The outside of this bath has been marbled, a popular treatment for this type of tub. Freestanding baths with ball-and-claw feet were much favoured in the early twentieth century, when built-in baths were considered unhygienic because they could harbour dust and dirt underneath them.

A corner bath takes up a little less space than a conventional one but does not really fit into the country house style. Baths set into an alcove are cosy and draught-free but should be designed carefully for easy cleaning. Building one or two steps up to the bath (if the ceiling height allows) makes this type of bath into a dramatic feature, as it can be sunken into the area below a false floor, with columns perhaps added on either side. Columns can be functional as well as decorative, as they can be made to open and house shelves for extra storage. This needs careful design, however, to have sufficient room for the door swing.

OTHER BATHROOM FITTINGS

A shower can be sited above the bath or housed in a separate cubicle, which can be bought as a self-contained unit or built into the structure of the room. An airing cupboard or alcove could be converted for the purpose. The shower tray is made of fireclay, acrylic, enamelled steel or composite synthetic in square, rectangular or triangular forms.

Some shower cubicles are available with 'Victorian'-style engraved glass, but most tend to look quite modern. To blend a shower into a country house style bathroom, therefore, the best approach is probably to make it as inconspicuous and plain as possible. A traditionally styled shower rose in a tiled alcove fitted with a simple glass door or a shower curtain could fit in reasonably well.

In terms of styling, a WC with a high-level cistern, such as the one on the right, is the most traditional, particularly if it has decorative brackets and a china or wooden cistern. However, a plain, functional, white, low-level WC also looks perfectly in keeping, especially if you fit it with a solid mahogany seat.

Before the installation of bathrooms in country houses, night-time sanitary arrangements in the bedroom were quite basic. Sometimes there were slop drawers under the bed which the long-suffering housemaid would have to empty in the morning. There also might be an armchair which housed a chamberpot under the seat which lifted up. An original one of these armchairs, or a reproduction, could be adapted to make an amusing surround for a modern WC.

The wash-basins can be wall-hung, set into the top of a vanity unit or pedestal-mounted so that the pedestal hides the pipework. Console basins are also available, in which the white ceramic basin is set into a ceramic surround on ceramic legs. It looks very much in keeping with country house style but is relatively expensive.

In order to make a bathroom seem less clinical and more like a room, one method of approach is to install the basins in a piece of old wood furniture such as a marble-topped washstand. Some people believe it

A modern tap would have been totally inappropriate for this delightful nineteenth century basin with integral soapdish and splashback.

A fine example of a traditional WC with a high-level wooden cistern. This would be very much in keeping with a late nineteenth century or early twentieth century style bathroom.

is sacrilege to alter an antique in this way, but it can be a good method of combining old and new – in the same way as old light fittings can be modified to take electric lights instead of candles.

The taps should be chosen to match the style of the room. Like baths, some basins are designed for the taps to be fitted directly to them, but with others they have to be chased into a wall above or behind the basin.

Heated towel rails are available in traditional styles and so are decorative as well as functional. The rail should obviously be positioned conveniently for the bath or shower but this could be at the foot of the bath instead of against the wall, which is a good way of breaking up the space. If you don't have a heated towel rail, an unheated wooden towel rack will also look very much in keeping.

Theatrical lighting around a mirror, which ensures shadow-free visibility, does not have to look modern and streamlined. Here it adds to the atmosphere of the bathroom, reminiscent of the opulent Beaux-Arts style of the nineteenth century.

STRONG BUT FLATTERING LIGHTING

It is sometimes difficult to combine efficient, up-to-date bathroom lighting satisfactorily with traditional country house style, but carefully chosen fittings and well thought-out lighting can solve this. Recessed lights give a pleasant, subtle light. Wall fixtures range from frosted glass globes to delicate fittings that provide general illumination. Ceiling fixtures vary in style and can be used in conjunction with task and accent lights.

Bathrooms are often woefully underlit – just one central fitting is rarely sufficient even in the smallest bathroom. They need task lighting that is gently flattering but is also strong enough for applying make-up or shaving. To prevent the lighting from looking utilitarian, focus the main task lighting on the mirror, and use fairly subdued general lighting elsewhere.

Lighting must be positioned carefully to avoid heavy shadows and it is therefore best to place it at the sides of a mirror as well as above. The light should ideally shine onto the user rather than the mirror itself. Suitable fittings for lighting mirrors include architectural strip lamps, wall lights or battens onto which balloon bulbs like theatre dressing-table lights have been fixed. There are also purpose-made fittings which fit over the top of a small mirror above a single basin or are incorporated into the mirror, giving a neat practical finish. Wall sconces on either side of the mirror give a very traditional look. A full-length or panoramic mirror should be lit by a length of tube. This could be run vertically along one or both sides of the mirror.

Light fittings should be chosen to minimize glare from the many shiny surfaces to be found in the bathroom such as mirrors, porcelain, ceramic tiles or glossy paintwork. Gold reflectors can be used to give a warm

White fittings look right in any period or style of country bathroom and are the only choice for a traditional bathroom. They are particularly versatile as they can be combined with any colour. The curved shower cubicle makes an interesting feature in this blue-and-white bathroom.

touch even to clinical white-tiled walls and floors. Wide-beam halogen fittings are a good choice to light mirrors. Narrow-beam versions placed over the bath or plants will create accents with the crisp white light which will also sparkle on water and the other reflective surfaces in the room.

Low-voltage downlighters are the safest choice of fitting to use near water, not only because of their voltage but also because the transformer itself acts as an isolating device. For showers, suitable light fittings are small sealed sources and certain low-voltage downlighters with sealed glass covers. Safety is a vital factor for all bathroom lighting, and regulations concerning this are strict, so check with your electrical contractor before making any irrevocable decisions about the bathroom lighting.

COLOUR OPTIONS

White fittings always look right in a country house style bathroom or cloakroom and, because they will not date, they allow the maximum flexibility for the colour scheme. White goes with anything: it combines well with a soft pastel scheme or can be thrown into relief against a dark wall colour. Or you can opt for an all-white scheme, using texture to prevent it from looking clinical.

In a nineteenth century style of decor, rich colours and finishes such as dark green and mahogany look appropriate, whereas eighteenth and twentieth century styles lend themselves to pretty pastels. To create a feeling of cohesion, *en suite* bathrooms can be decorated to tie in with the scheme in the adjoining bedroom.

PRACTICAL WALLS WITH A PERIOD FEEL

Ceramic tiles are still the most practical surface for the walls of a bathroom. The huge variety available means that they do not have to appear in the white favoured earlier this century and can easily be adapted to a style or theme. A botanical theme, for example, could be picked up in a random repeat of a flower or leaf design among plain tiles. A strong Victorian feel could be introduced with the use of the very distinctive tiles that were produced in that period. Tiling can be taken up to about chair rail height, or right up to the ceiling, though this can sometimes seem a little chilly and uninviting, and makes the room prone to echoes.

Eggshell or silk finish paint is the best paint for a bathroom or cloakroom, unless it is going to receive unusually heavy wear and tear or condensation, in which case there are special paints that have been developed for the purpose. Paint effects work well in a country house style bathroom, as the oil-based glazes can withstand the steamy atmosphere, and the textured finish they give adds subtle interest.

Stencilling lends itself to bathrooms as much as to bedrooms (see page 156) and could look particularly pretty in the form of a soft border at chair rail or cornice (crown molding) level. Freehand or stencilled all-over flower designs would look delightful in a country house bathroom or cloakroom, as in the cloakroom shown on the right. (Be sure to protect the stencilling with a matt acrylic varnish so it will be washable.) As in kitchens, stencilling on tiles, though feasible using special paint, is not recommended because the paint will not withstand frequent washing.

Murals too can be used to make a stunning feature, whether created from ceramic tiles or specially painted.

A striking mirror sets off a handsome console basin in this unusual cloakroom. The antique shaving stand is a charming addition that would work equally well in a bathroom.

Because of the steam, the only wallpaper that is suitable in a bathroom is vinyl. Fortunately, it is so much improved these days that it is almost indistinguishable from ordinary wallpaper, and there are many designs suitable for country house style. Even with vinyl, however, damp can be a problem, so ventilation of the room is essential, and splashbacks are important. These can be made of tiles, mirror, tongue-and-groove panelling or plexiglas, a clear perspex screen.

Mirrors can be very effectively used in a bathroom to increase the apparent length or width of the room. It should be placed to reflect something interesting such as a view of the garden. A mirrored alcove could be lined with glass shelves.

Marble is wonderfully luxurious, and although it is expensive and weighty its traditional associations ensure that it will always look right in a country house

bathroom. For the same reason, a marble paint effect is perfect here (see page 169). Terracotta, granite or slate tiles could also be used. Tongue and groove panelling, painted with eggshell paint, is another finish compatible with country house style. It can be positioned to chair rail height to hide the pipework or cistern.

Bathrooms and cloakrooms are the perfect place to indulge some more original decorative ideas. Instead of the usual wallpaper the walls could be covered with prints, posters, collections of art postcards or old documents and then sealed with polyurethane varnish to protect them. Don't forget the ceiling, which will be in full view when you are lying in the bath.

A cloakroom, which will not be used as much as a bathroom, lends itself to fantasy decoration – perhaps a map of the world, a collection of cartoons or a shell grotto with silvered shell-shaped wall lights.

Subtle ochre, terracotta and dove grey were used to decorate the walls and floor of this cloakroom. The ancient-looking stencil design is actually modern and was inspired by a motif on a Provençal woodblock.

Here a dramatically pretty effect has been achieved by draping fabric from the ceiling over small fabric-covered brackets on either side of the bath to form a canopy in the French style.

A vinyl-tile floor designed to look like marble is in keeping with this period-style bathroom, with its marble fireplace and clawfoot tub – and this flooring is not cold to walk on like marble is. The shower, too, though completely modern, has a classic look that blends successfully into the room.

FLOORING IDEAS

In a country house style bathroom, a carpeted floor is warm, welcoming and luxurious. It is now possible to buy cotton loop pile carpet that is mounted onto a waterproof bitumen backing that is both moisture- and stain- resistant. A pure wool carpet is to be avoided as it will smell when wet. Wall-to-wall carpet should not be permanently fixed down in case access is needed to pipework under the floorboards or the bath or bidet overflows.

Marble and ceramic tiles are cold and potentially slippery underfoot but these days vinyls give virtually the same look without these disadvantages. Sealed cork is pleasantly warm underfoot but sealed floorboards tend to be noisy and unwelcoming and so need washable rugs. For a tiled or vinyl floor that needs regular cleaning, the addition of a discreetly positioned drain hole in a corner will make washing easier and will take care of any accidental spillage from the bath, basin or shower.

FABRIC IN THE BATHROOM

If privacy is a factor, curtains combined with a very fine microblind colour-matched to the room, or with a laminated lace panel such as that shown opposite, could look highly decorative. Other alternatives include internal shutters, varnished wooden Venetian blinds, a fixed screen, wooden lattice or decorative opaque or coloured glass panels.

A roller blind (shade) is one of the most popular treatments for a bathroom window. It can be made to fit into a country house style better by the addition of a prettily shaped lambrequin constructed from MDF (medium density fibreboard) or chipboard (particleboard) and then painted or covered in fabric. This would also cut out any draughts.

A lambrequin – a stiff, shaped pelmet that continues down the sides of the window – could be particularly appropriate for a slightly masculine style decor, but most curtain styles can be adapted to the country house style of bathroom. A curtain or blind

A delicate, laminated lace blind is a charming and traditional way of providing privacy in this period-style bathroom. The towels with embroidered monograms add to the look.

to match the wallpaper above the tiles can look very attractive but it is important not to use delicate fabrics. Cotton is ideal for a bathroom.

Bathroom curtains do not have to be particularly extravagant or fussy. Simple crisp white linen curtains on a pole or track or even made out of linen sheets or lining material will look good and can be linked into the colour scheme of an adjoining bedroom with a scalloped edging or plain or patterned border to match.

Gathered muslin looped over a pole and caught back at the sides with bows or rosettes gives a soft look, and paired curtains of calico or ticking look simple and smart. Other fabrics in keeping with a country house style would be faded linens, old chintzes or even damask on poles.

In addition to the window treatment, you could always drape a fabric canopy above a rolltop bath, for a dramatically pretty effect, as in the photograph on the left.

FITTING IN SOME FURNITURE

There always seems to be a surprising amount to store in a bathroom, but resist the temptation to install modern built-in units, because they might ruin the country house bathroom effect. The obvious place for cupboards is below the wash-basin. The vanity unit could be finished in plain white, a decorative paint finish or natural wood. A rich mahogany or a pale limed oak would look equally suitable. A deep box frame built-in around a sheet of mirror on the wall above the basins will not only create a recess for the mirror but will also allow fluorescent lights to be set behind panels of sandblasted glass for good light and a neat finish.

THE PRINT ROOM

A 'print room' theme, based on the eighteenth century vogue for pasting engravings on the walls (see pages 23 and 24), then linking them with paper bows, tasselled ropes, swags, etc, would work well in a cloakroom. Try to relate their size and position to the scale of the room, and position them symmetrically where possible.

Coloured prints could be used, but black-and-white line engravings of classical or architectural subjects are more traditional and have more impact. The classical sobriety contrasts well with the frivolous borders and ropes. For an antique effect, photocopy the engravings then paint the paper lightly with cold tea or an antiquing glaze.

If space allows, a small armchair and perhaps a prettily painted two-tier table, or a small wine table near the bath, would contribute to the atmosphere of comfort and luxury in a bathroom or cloakroom. A large mahogany chest with perhaps the addition of a dressing table mirror might be another interesting addition, while an old painted wardrobe or large freestanding cupboard is ideal for storing towels and bathroom clutter. A cheval mirror (an old-fashioned, freestanding, full-length mirror) would be perfectly suited to the style.

LUXURY ACCESSORIES

The Greek word 'to bathe' also meant 'to drive sadness from the mind' and country house bathrooms certainly do that. Accessories should be chosen to reinforce the feeling of luxury and relaxation. For example, it's not just the colour of towels that is important but also their texture and absorbency. Egyptian cotton towels are soft and very absorbent.

Many traditional towel rails, soap dishes, shaving stands and other accessories are available today, both antique and reproduction, and look fabulous in this style of bathroom or cloakroom. Thoughtful extras such as toothbrush and mug holders and bath trays with sponges, soap and pretty bottles can make all the difference.

Suitable decorative objects might include a pretty flower-patterned ewer and basin, ceramic or glass storage jars, framed prints in keeping with the overall theme or style, and baskets containing soap or bath pearls. Instead of sheets of mirror glass or contemporary framed mirrors, new mirror glass could be fixed into old painted or gilded picture frames for a traditional but highly decorative touch. Receptacles for rubbish and laundry are often last-minute additions to a bathroom. There are some quite decorative laundry baskets to be found.

This welcoming bathroom is furnished very much like a sitting room, with a fireplace, chest and comfortable armchair for bathtime conversation. There is, however, a risk of water spillage from the bath or shower mixer after use.

THE CONSERVATORY

DEVELOPMENT OF THE CONSERVATORY

One outcome of the eighteenth century enthusiasm for travel was an enormous interest in exotic plant specimens, with many travellers bringing back cuttings to propagate at home. A lot of these specimens needed protection from the frost in order to survive through the winter, and it was for this purpose that the first glasshouses were built in the eighteenth century. Known as orangeries, they were usually constructed in the classical style with broad windows between columns and solid roofs.

The orangery became an essential for all grand houses in Britain and was also fashionable in Europe and in America. It was either rectangular or semicircular with a central pavilion. In the spring, after the frosts passed, the orange trees and other fruit trees, in their containers, would be removed from the orangery and placed on the terrace of the house, and the empty orangery used for summer entertaining.

Towards the end of the eighteenth century the conservatory really came into its own, as great advances were made in the manufacture of glass. It became possible to build complex and delicate iron frameworks that allowed glass to be the dominant element, and some magnificent conservatories were built with glass roofs.

In the early nineteenth century, conservatories became increasingly popular and were still used for housing plants and entertaining. New designs allowed the maximum light to reach the plants, though many of the constructions were so delicate that they did not survive very long.

Conservatories continued to be fashionable into the early twentieth century and were sometimes used for events such as balls and tea parties. In the 1920s the garden room, or sun room, became popular and many smaller country houses were extended in this way. These were rather frowned on in grander circles and in any case the conservatory began to be viewed as rather passé. Many were converted into open loggias, and then gradually both the conservatory and the loggia fell out of favour. One reason for this was that the advent of central heating in the main part of the house made the unheated conservatory a chilly and unwelcoming spot.

In the 1970s the conservatory became fashionable again. Now that it could be effectively glazed, heated and ventilated, it could provide valuable, light-filled, extra living space as well as housing plants. A number of specialist companies sprang up who could provide a complete design service – usually in keeping with the architectural style of the existing house. Today there is no sign of the popularity of the conservatory waning.

When the weather was mild enough, eighteenth century orangeries (the forerunners of conservatories) were emptied of their contents and used for entertaining – a function that has continued since then. Today, this spacious, high-ceilinged conservatory would make an equally romantic and practical setting for large-scale entertaining.

PLANNING THE CONSERVATORY

The interior of the conservatory needs to be considered at an early stage. One common fault is to put in too many doors or doors in awkward places which leaves very little room for arranging furniture satisfactorily and not much wall space.

The function of the room will dictate the furniture and materials to a large extent. A conservatory can fulfil any of a variety of roles, including doubling as a pretty dining room, an extension of a kitchen to provide a breakfast area, a relaxing family room, a children's playroom, a garden room or orangery or even a working studio for a designer or artist.

It might be possible to put the whole kitchen in a conservatory providing it is generally well shaded from the sun. A lean-to design works best as this provides a solid wall against which storage cabinets, oven and appliances can be placed. If the hob is included in this line-up, providing ventilation or extractor fans will be easier. Double glazing is essential in a conservatory used as a kitchen, to limit condensation and keep in as much heat as possible.

North light with no direct sunlight would be the ideal orientation for a working studio for an artist or designer, but closely fitted blinds would help to eliminate glare if this was not possible.

NIGHT-TIME LIGHTING

One of the difficulties of lighting a conservatory is that a great deal of light comes in during the day but at night it goes out into the blackness beyond. Strong lights cause harsh reflections against the glass, so several low-strength lights will give a softer, more comfortable light than just a few bright bulbs.

A decorative cast iron grille which covers the heating duct, allowing the heat to escape into the room, is visible in the floor of this conservatory extension, featuring a profusion of summer plants and a handsome birdcage.

Probably the prettiest lighting of all would be provided by candles, but although they are a lovely option for a special dinner party, they are not practical for everyday use. However, halogen low-voltage lighting produces a glow similar to candlelight and can be neatly fitted into the roof structure to light the room below.

Victorian conservatories were lit with oil lamps (later converted to gas or electricity) as well as candles, and it is possible to find original versions of these or good reproductions of hanging lanterns or wall brackets which could be fixed to the solid wall. Another nineteenth century fashion that would still look delightful for an evening party was to mass Chinese lanterns on wires across the room.

Because furniture and plants in a conservatory are often rearranged, the lighting plan should have in-built flexibility. Avoid uplighters, as the roof panes would bounce back glaring light into the space, and conventional spotlights which would look completely out of keeping. Hanging fittings can be unsatisfactory as they often interfere with the blinds but a stylized chandelier hung from the roof can make a stunning centrepiece which could set the theme for the whole scheme.

HEATING AND VENTILATION

Heating is usually supplied by an extension of the main system for the house which runs in a duct covered with decorative cast iron grilles to allow the heat to escape around the edge of the conservatory. An example is shown in the conservatory above. Underfloor heating can also be provided. Although it is inexpensive to run and invisible and it leaves the floor and wall space completely clear, it does take time to respond to existing weather conditions, which is not ideal for the occupants or the plants. A cast-iron stove can look decorative in a conservatory but not all plants can survive the fumes given off by the wood or coal.

A narrow shelf above lace-curtained double doors provides clever night lighting for this conservatory. Low-voltage halogen lights have been set into the bottom of the shelf so that the light shines through the lace and nearby plants. Meanwhile, the top of the shelf holds candles and night-lights (votives) in coloured glass jars, creating a wonderfully romantic atmosphere.

Ventilation is a vital consideration as so much heat can build up in a glass room. If the construction does not get a great deal of sun, at least a third of the windows will need to open – vertically sliding sashes or centre pivoted windows are best. Doors hung on hinges that permit them to be folded outwards at 180 degrees so they can be hooked back against the frame of the conservatory would be sufficient. Where there is more sunlight, a roof ventilation system is needed. There are some modern systems which are electrically operated and incorporate thermostats and automatic time controls. In some instances a simple electric fan suspended from the ceiling of the conservatory would be sufficient.

FLOORING POSSIBILITIES

Apart from the glass, the floorcovering will be the biggest surface area in the conservatory and should be considered as an integral part of the scheme. This is an area that will receive considerable wear and tear. People will be going in and out, to and from the garden, and the very strong sunlight can fade or rot some more delicate materials so a durable, practical flooring is essential. It must also be frostproof.

The floors of nineteenth century conservatories were usually of flagstones. Gothic revival versions had medieval-style floors made of small terracotta tiles of various colours arranged in patterns or encaustic tiles where the designs were part of the manufacturing process.

Among the most popular choices today are quarry tiles. Very tough and frostproof, these are available in various earthy colours and also black and blue. They need to be sealed, which darkens the colour, a factor to bear in mind when choosing them. They would look particularly nice if two or three colours were arranged in a geometric

pattern. Encaustic tiles will also look wonderful in a conservatory, though their price means they are mainly restricted to conservation work.

Natural clay tiles, though suitable for halls (if sealed), are not frostproof and so are not recommended for conservatories. Some glazed floor tiles are frostproof but others are not. They do not need sealing and come in a vast range of colours and patterns. Bear in mind that they are very slippery when wet. Mosaic, terrazzo or inlaid marble flooring are other attractive possibilities.

Limestone, sandstone and slate would all make durable and attractive flooring for a conservatory, and are available with many subtle variations of colour. Marble is slippery when wet so would not be a good idea if you will have a lot of plants that need watering.

Quality vinyls imitating any of these effects, or plain or patterned linoleum, might also look good, and they are very practical. An attractive rug can make the conservatory look cosier and more welcoming and can often help pull the decorative scheme together. A natural flooring such as seagrass will also give a softer look, while rush matting is suitable because it must not be allowed to get too dry and so actually benefits from regular sprinkling with water.

BLINDS AND CURTAINS

In addition to good ventilation, the roof also needs some sort of cover to provide shade, though obviously this must be designed not to obstruct the roof ventilators. Roller or

Conservatory floors can be plain or patterned. Here quarry tiles in black and terracotta are laid in an attractive diamond pattern.

Natural materials are suited to conservatories, and here pinoleum blinds filter the sunlight effectively. A magnificent ficus surrounded by a cushion-covered wicker bench seat is the focal point of the room.

ENCAUSTIC TILES

One of the earliest types of tile ever made, encaustic tiles were traditional in Victorian and Edwardian conservatories, as well as entrance halls, corridors and patios. They had originally been hand-made by Cistercian monks in medieval times, and the technique was rediscovered during the Gothic revival of the nineteenth century. A few companies still make them today. Usually inlaid with geometric or heraldic patterns, they come in natural colours with blue and black. They provide the perfect opportunity to introduce a decorative feature and an element of period style.

Roman blinds (shades) can be used but pinoleum (pinewood sawn into thin reeds which are sewn together and finished with clothbound edges, shown on page 185) is the traditional type of conservatory blind. It filters the sun very effectively and, as it is stiff, does not sag as much as fabric blinds.

Another solution is an electrically operated Venetian blind which is fixed outside the conservatory roof. The system automatically adjusts the angle of the slats according to the strength and angle of the sun.

Curtains can be fitted to give a cosier feel in a conservatory used as a family room but the framework would almost certainly need to be adjusted in order to fit the necessary tracks neatly. They are usually fitted in pairs looped back against the posts between windows, with the same fabric gathered and stretched between cords in the roof. Any fabric used must be able to withstand strong sunlight and humidity.

SUITABLE FURNITURE

Materials that might be damaged by a moist atmosphere or might create glare should be avoided, and so strong, matt finishes are probably the best choice for furniture. Painted furniture thrives in the humidity. Sturdy natural materials such as wrought iron, timber and wicker with table tops in slate and marble and cushions made of cottons and linens work particularly well. However the room is used, one big table would be a useful addition. To soften the look or dress it up for evening, the table could be covered with a suitable style of durable fabric such as a Provençal print or Indian cotton.

Chairs or benches could be made of timber, wrought iron, galvanized steel, wicker, rattan (which can be given a variety of distressed finishes), or bamboo. For a family room, sofas and armchairs in wicker

could be added, or for a garden room choose cast-iron chairs or benches with nature-inspired motifs. Cushions could be in feather or down with loose covers or foam-filled squab cushions, while fabrics could vary from natural-coloured to hand-painted linen and cotton or small kelims.

WELL-CHOSEN ACCESSORIES

Wire-framed jardinières were used a great deal in nineteenth century country house conservatories and would conjure up a Victorian feel to the room. A pair of semi-circular ones placed back-to-back and filled with plants makes an imposing centrepiece. In a formal conservatory, classic containers such as Versailles boxes look right, but varying sizes and types of ceramic containers such as Oriental or Mediterranean styles will also work in country house style. Wicker and terracotta are also suitable for most styles of conservatory, can be seen in the conservatory on the left.

Mirrors with gilt or painted frames appear to increase the sense of space and reflect light, which looks particularly attractive in candlelight. In a classical style of conservatory, architectural definition can be introduced with columns to break up the space or low columns used as plant stands. This style blends well with contemporary wrought iron furniture as well as more traditional wooden console tables or stone benches. Where wall space allows, a trompe l'oeil mural could give the impression of a vista beyond.

Comfort is a priority in this pretty blue and white conservatory where a pine-framed antique sofa is piled with bolsters and cushions and, like the two armchairs, covered in a cotton fabric. A tall, rustic candlestick, wicker and terracotta containers and a pleasing flower-patterned rug add to the easy informality of the space.

INDEX

PICTURE ACKNOWLEDGEMENTS

The Publisher should like to thank the following sources for their kind permission to reproduce the photographs in this book:

Amtico 176 left;

Arcaid /Richard Bryant 16 left, 22-23, 33 top right, 39, 40-41 (by kind permission of The Mount Vernon Ladies' Association of the Union), 42, 43, 49, 53, 80, 91, 149, 165, 166-167, **/Jeremy Cockayne** 92-93, 96-97 (Axel Vervoordt, Castle of 's Gravenwezel, Belgium), **/Mark Fiennes** 19, **/Ken Kirkwood** 158, 174-175, **/Lucinda Lambton** 102-103, 150;

Robert Harding Picture Library /Mike Newton 184-185;

Robert Harding Picture Library /IPC Magazines Ltd. 84-85, **/Simon Brown** 152-153, **/Christopher Drake** 24 top left, 60 bottom left, 167 bottom right, **/Tim Goffe** 176-177, **/Tom Leighton** 3, **/James Merrell** 89, 132-133, **/Hugh Palmer** 185 bottom right, **/Peter Rauter** 183 top right, 186-187, **/Trevor Richards** 1, 134-135, 160-161, **/Simon Upton** 78 left, **/Fritz von der Schulenburg** 172-173, **/Andreas von Einsiedel** 56, 82 top left;

The Interior Archive /Tim Beddow 6, 32-33, 72-73, 73 top right, 141, 144-145, 148, 177 top right, **/Tim Clinch** 104-5, **/James Mortimer** 30-31, 68, **/C Simon Sykes** 9, 10 left, 11, 21 top right, 24-25, 26-27, 28-29, 34-35, 50, 54-55, 107, 111, 114 top left, 124-125, 128, 139 **/Simon Upton** 71, **/Fritz von der Schulenburg** 14-15, 16-17, 20-21, 36-37, 67, 82-83, 86, 101, 104 left, 117, 127, 129, 131 top right, 146, 147 top and bottom, 154-155, 157, 170;

Anthony James & Son Ltd. 74;

Martin Moore and Company 113;

The National Trust Photographic Library /Geoffrey Frosh 12-13;

Ianthe Ruthven 44-45, 69, 125 top right;

Elizabeth Whiting and Associates 2, 4-5, 7, 15 right, 52, 54 left, 57, 58, 60-61, 62 top left, 62-63, 64, 70, 75, 76, 78-79, 94-95, 95 bottom right, 97 top right, 98 top left, 98-99, 100, 108 top left, 108-109, 112, 114-115, 116, 118 top left, 118-119, 120, 121, 123, 130-131, 134 top left, 136-137, 138, 142, 143, 144 top left, 153 bottom right, 159, 161 top right, 162, 168-169, 171 top right, 172 bottom left, 175 top right, 178-179, 181, 182-183.